Silk Painting

Silk Painting

Step-by-step techniques and ideas
for colour and design

COLLEEN WESTE

GREENHOUSE

Greenhouse
Penguin Books Australia Ltd
487 Maroondah Highway, PO Box 257
Ringwood, Victoria 3134, Australia
Penguin Books Ltd
Harmondsworth, Middlesex, England
Viking Penguin, A Division of Penguin Books USA Inc.
375 Hudson Street, New York, New York 10014, USA
Penguin Books Canada Limited
10 Alcorn Avenue, Toronto, Ontario, Canada M4V 3B2
Penguin Books (N.Z.) Ltd
182-190 Wairau Road, Auckland 10, New Zealand

First published by Penguin Books Australia Ltd 1993

10 9 8 7 6 5 4 3 2 1

Produced by Viking O'Neil
56 Claremont Street, South Yarra, Victoria 3141, Australia
A Division of Penguin Books Australia Ltd

Design by Pauline McClenahan
Cover photograph and photographs facing page 69
by Shane McClenahan
Typeset in Caxton Light by EMS Typesetting
Printed and bound through Bookbuilders Limited, Hong Kong

National Library of Australia
Cataloguing-in-Publication data

Weste, Colleen.
Silk painting.

Bibliography.
Includes index.
ISBN 0 86436 404 0.

1. Silk painting – Technique. I. Title.

746.6

Rosella Flight by Liz Darby is illustrated on the half title page
Opal Patterns by Colleen Weste is illustrated facing the title page

CONTENTS

SECTION 4 *Projects*

SECTION 5 *Appendices*

INTRODUCTION

The art of painting on silk is fascinating to many people. The rich lustre of silk and the joy of applying vibrant and beautiful dyes in a simple way appeal to the beginner, and continue to hold their appeal as your knowledge progresses, and you start to try more complex techniques for colouring the fabric.

With this book, I aim to teach you the basic methods of silk painting, to help you create your own designs, and, most important of all, to show you how to develop your own awareness of the world around you.

The book is divided into five sections. The first is a comprehensive introduction to the materials and equipment needed for silk painting. Then follows an outline of the basic principles of colour and design. You can derive endless inspiration from nature, so I have also included a chapter on photographing the world around you so you can begin to see nature in new ways and collect reference material. The third section discusses the techniques of silk painting in detail. Taking examples from nature and the environment and with the help of some notable artists, I illustrate how to interpret Australian wildflowers, birds and landscape on silk.

In the fourth section I suggest ways in which you might use your silk painting and give some simple projects, as well as explaining how to sew with silk.

Finally, there is a reference section with suggestions for further reading, brief biographies of the artists and a list of stockists and suppliers.

The book is illustrated with colour photographs and beautiful design ideas, which should inspire painters and textile artists and, I hope, encourage those who have never painted on silk to try their hand at it. Beginners should be able to understand the straightforward explanation of these techniques and step-by-step illustrations, gain confidence, and do their own rewarding work, while the more experienced will find new and advanced ways of using this art form. I hope that you will find your own way of capturing nature in this exciting and beautiful medium.

SECTION 1

Equipment and Materials

Silk

Silk is a natural fibre obtained from silk moths. The thread is reeled off in long filaments from the cocoons formed by the larvae. Silk filament is fine and smooth, and it has a natural lustre and gloss that makes it ideal for dyeing and decorative painting. Its characteristics are strength, warmth, wearability, softness and comfort.

Silk was first manufactured in China as long ago as 3000 BC and painting on silk is almost as old as the use of silk itself, and can be traced as far back as the Chou Dynasty (1027-249 BC).

Silk became a highly prized commodity in Europe and to reach this market travelled along the Silk Road, a 10,000 kilometre journey from China, through central Asia, India and Syria to Rome. The journey took six to eight years and was extremely hazardous and difficult, but for the prize of silk it was considered worthwhile. China managed to protect its monopoly for two thousand years by surrounding silk and its origins and manufacture with extreme secrecy; death was the penalty for betraying its secrets or for exporting the precious silkworm. The secret of silk escaped from China when, in AD 552, the Roman Emperor Justinian ordered two Byzantine monks living in China to act as spies. They successfully smuggled silkworm eggs out of China, and this was the beginning of silk production in Europe.

Italy and France developed major silk industries of their own; Germany and Prussia manufactured silk for a short while in the eighteenth century, and Germany produced parachute silk from 1934-45. There were attempts to establish sericulture in England and the United States, but with limited success. In Australia in the 1870s it was believed that silk production could become an important industry, but this did not succeed. Even today, China is still the world leader in silk production. However, Japan claims a higher raw silk yield from cocoons as a result of their improved technology.

The way in which the silk is woven determines its thickness and texture. Silk is graded by the mommie. This is a traditional Japanese measurement for both silk and pearls and it represents the weight of the fabric per square metre. (A mommie is approximately 4.33 grams.) Silks vary from 5 mommie (or 20 g per square metre) to 140 mommie (600 g per square metre) or more. The higher the number of mommie is, the denser the silk.

The following silks are suitable for painting and for the projects in this book.

Pongee or paj

A smooth, shiny, fine silk, ideal for beginners. It is excellent for scarves, linings and for experiments in painting. It usually comes in 5, 6 and 6.5 mommie.

Habutai

A plain-woven, shiny silk ideal for scarves, garments, accessories, cushions, furnishings, wall hangings or pictures. Density ranges from 8 to 16 mommie, and this fabric is sold in widths of 95–112 cm.

My Kind of Country by Thel Merry (see page 44 for a detailed description).

Pelicans by Liz Darby (see page 43 for a detailed description).

Contrasting blends of vivid colour by Colleen Weste.

Parrots and Waratahs by Jillian Townley (see page 43 for a detailed description).

Twill

A strong fabric with a diagonal twill weave, which gives it more sheen. Used for ties, clothing, scarves and furnishings. It comes in densities from 10 to 17 mommie.

Crêpe de Chine

A plain fabric with a crêpe weave that produces a characteristic surface texture. It is soft and drapes well, and so it is recommended for exclusive clothes, lingerie and scarves. However, it does soak up the dye and will shrink somewhat when wet, so it must be washed before making up.

Crêpe de Chine comes in densities of 10 to 18 mommie.

Satin

A fabric with a warp-faced weave that gives it a characteristic smooth, lustrous surface and a rich, slippery feel. It is mostly used for lingerie and evening clothes.

Satin comes in 12, 19 and 23 mommie, and it may have a crêpe backing.

Douppioni

This is a thicker, textured fabric woven from the filament of the wild tusser moth. Sometimes known as 'raw', 'tusser', 'tussah' or 'tussore' silk. A characteristic is its 'slubs' or irregularities. Douppioni is suitable for garments, cushions and screens.

Douppioni ranges in density from 15 to 36 mommie.

Georgette, organza and chiffon

These are very fine, transparent fabrics. Georgette comes in either plain or crêpe weave and, because it is so soft and drapes beautifully, it is used for blouses, dresses and scarves. Organza is used in a similar way, but its characteristic stiffness makes it ideal for articles such as collars and blouses.

Georgette usually has a density of 5 to 10 mommie, while organza is usually about 8 mommie.

Chiffon is thin and sheer and has a very open weave. It can be difficult to handle and sew, but it has excellent draping qualities.

Care of silk

Silk can be washed by hand or dry-cleaned.

Hand wash silk gently in warm, soapy water for a few minutes in a gentle detergent designed for wool and silk, not in a harsh alkali. Rinse in warm to cool water, squeezing out excess moisture. Steam iron while still very damp. Some silks have size or dressing in them. Before painting, they should therefore be washed in warm, soapy water to allow the dyes and gutta to penetrate the fibres more thoroughly.

Dyes

Several types of dyes and paints are suitable for silk painting. I recommend that you stay with one class of dye and become familiar with the product, the method for successful application and the range of colours available. You are then free to concentrate your energy on your silk art.

It is helpful to know the difference between paints and dyes. Fabric paints are essentially pigments suspended in a resin base. The paint sits on the surface of the weave and is bonded to the fabric by means of a hot iron. Dyes penetrate the fabric and bond to the actual fibre itself. Paints can be applied to almost any fabric, whereas dyes are specialised for particular fibres. Paints are opaque, while dyes are transparent. Dyes leave the cloth with a softer handle, whereas paints tend to stiffen the cloth if they are applied thickly. Dyes come in several categories:

- vegetable dyes
- acid-based dyes
- reactive dyes
- napthol dyes
- soluble vat dyes
- disperse dyes.

In this book I concentrate on the French acid-based dyes, the cold fibre-reactive dyes, suitable fabric paints and the liquid-fixed dyes, but all the dyes mentioned above, except the disperse dyes, can nevertheless be used for silk painting. The techniques I describe can be applied on all protein and cellulose fibres.

Acid-based dyes

The French silk painting dyes are the most popular around the world. They come in a range of brilliant colours, and are transparent, so that when one is painted over another they blend and shimmer together. All can be intermixed, and they may be diluted with water or a diluent that contains alcohol. Dupont recommend diluting the dyes with one of the following solutions:

- half water + half alcohol or diluent
- 20 cc concentrated diluent + 980 cc water.

For wool, lighten the colours by half with the first of the above solutions.

A thickening agent can be used to slow down the spreading of the dye and for silk screening. The standard proportion is 20 per cent thickener to 80 per cent dye. These dyes are steam-fixed in order to make them colour-fast. Their colour fastness when washed and exposed to the light is then good.

The brands available include Dupont, Pebeo, Elbesoie and Princecolour.

Cold fibre-reactive dyes

These dyes are popular because they are easy to use, especially on wool. In Australia they are sold in powder form. Fixation is achieved by steaming or wrapping the fabric in plastic overnight, which causes a chemical bonding to take place. Colours are extremely fast to light and washing. The range of colours is

A selection of dyes for painting on silk.

limited compared with the French dyes. Brand names are Drimalan, Procion, Lanasol, Silk Express.

You will notice that, as the dyes dry on the silk, the colours seem to dull somewhat. However, after steaming the colours will be bright and permanent, and the lustrous quality of the silk will show through.

Fabric paints

The several paints on the market have varying consistencies. Some of the brand names are Dekasilk (from Germany), Imprefix, Acrylique (from Dupont), Setacolour (from Pebeo). They can be diluted with water or white for pastel colours. Remember, they are suitable for all fabrics. In my experience, the colours are not as vibrant as the steam-fixed dyes, but they have useful applications.

The alizarine-based paints are fixed with an iron. Iron the silk on the reverse side, with or without an ironing cloth, for 15-20 seconds, taking care not to burn the fabric. Dupont recommend fixing at 150°C for 5 minutes in a frying pan or the oven. The fabric can then be washed or dry-cleaned.

Liquid-fixed dyes

Some dyes are designed to be fixed with a liquid fixative. For these, soak the fabric in the fixative for approximately one hour, or according to instructions. Then rinse in warm water to remove the fixative and any excess colour.

Two brand name are Orient Express and Princefix.

Steam-fixed dyes

As I mentioned earlier, the acid-based French dyes require steam for fixing and the reactive dyes may also be steam-fixed. Specialist shops run a steaming service that is relatively cheap, but if your prefer to do your own, the vertical steamer from France illustrated on this page is excellent but very expensive. It takes fabric up to 1.3 m wide and 30 m in length.

A box-type steamer is made locally and is a good investment only if your are doing a lot of dyeing. It has an electric element and can take approximately 20 m of fabric.

It is possible to steam your own silk at home using a pressure cooker or steamer saucepan. Roll the silk fabric into a parcel between layers of paper – use white butcher's paper, tissue, kitchen paper, old newsprint or something similar. Never allow silk to touch silk. Wrap the parcel with two layers of foil and seal thoroughly so no water can seep in. Alternatively you can seal it in an oven bag.

You can steam the wrapped silk in one of two ways:

- place the parcel in a pressure cooker with a trivet and steam under pressure for 50 minutes, or
- use a steamer or double saucepan, and seal and steam for 1 hour 20 minutes.

It is important, if you are using a steamer or saucepan, to keep the water at a rolling boil to ensure there is sufficient heat. When the time is up, remove the pan from the heat, and check a corner of the fabric for fixation by dipping it in water. Rinse following the instructions on the following page.

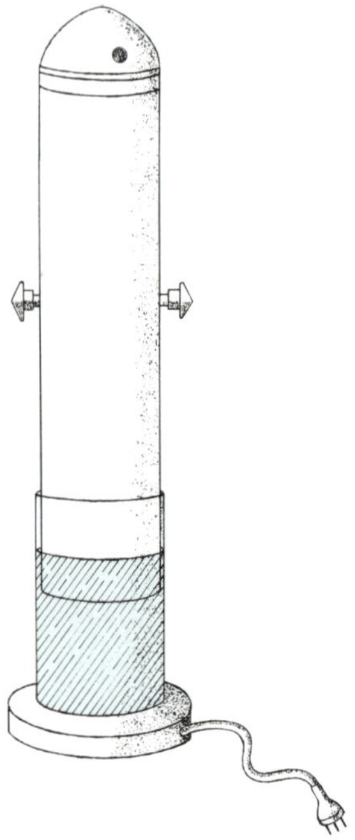

Vertical steamer will take up to 30 metres of fabric.

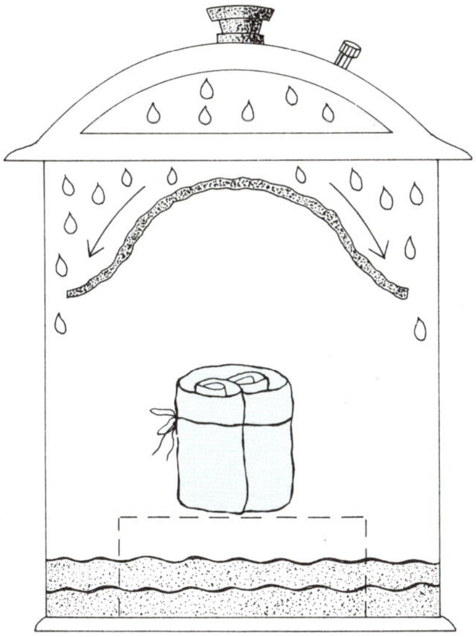

Steaming silk in a pressure cooker.

Washing

You will notice that after steaming the colours are more vibrant, and the silk is softer and has a lustrous sheen. Before washing, you may wish to test a strip of the fabric to check that colours are fixed. If the colour runs and the silk colour pales, remove the fabric from the water immediately and repeat the steaming process.

Wash the fabric by putting it in warm soapy water, using a non-alkali soap, for approximately two minutes. Rinse until the water clears. If there is any colour in the water, it should only be excess dye, so keep rinsing until the water is clear.

Squeeze excess moisture out of the silk, and hang it to dry for a few minutes only. Then steam iron (on a wool setting) while the fabric is still very damp. If the silk has dried, dampen it again well before ironing.

Safety

All chemicals are hazardous and certain safety procedures should always be followed and sensible precautions taken. Dyes such as the acid-based French silk painting dyes are diluted in liquid form and are, therefore, less toxic than the reactive or napthol dyes that come in powder form.

- When handling dyes, always wear protective gloves and, when you are using powder dyes, a mask is also recommended.
- Store your dyes in a dark cupboard away from direct heat.
- Work in a ventilated area. The steam-fixed dyes are odourless, but the latex-based guttas can occasionally affect people with sensitivities.
- Exercise the common sense you would use for household cleaners, and keep dye materials away from children.
- Do not use dye equipment for cooking or preparing food.
- For further information contact The Australian Forum for Textile Arts (TAFTA) or the Crafts Council of Australia for publications on occupational hazards in the arts.

Frames

It is best to have the silk fabric stretched out and raised above the work surface for painting. Several types of frame are suitable.

Adjustable pin frame

On this frame the silk slips onto fine sharp pins (called 'picot' edging in France) spaced 1 cm apart. There is a protective lid for safety. The pin ends are then pulled taut and fastened with wing nuts. The advantage of this frame is that it can be adjusted to take a piece of silk from 10 cm to 2 m long. The fabric can be tightened easily with the wing nuts and blocks if the silk sags (it has a tendency to stretch when wet). The frame also folds away compactly when not in use or for transportation.

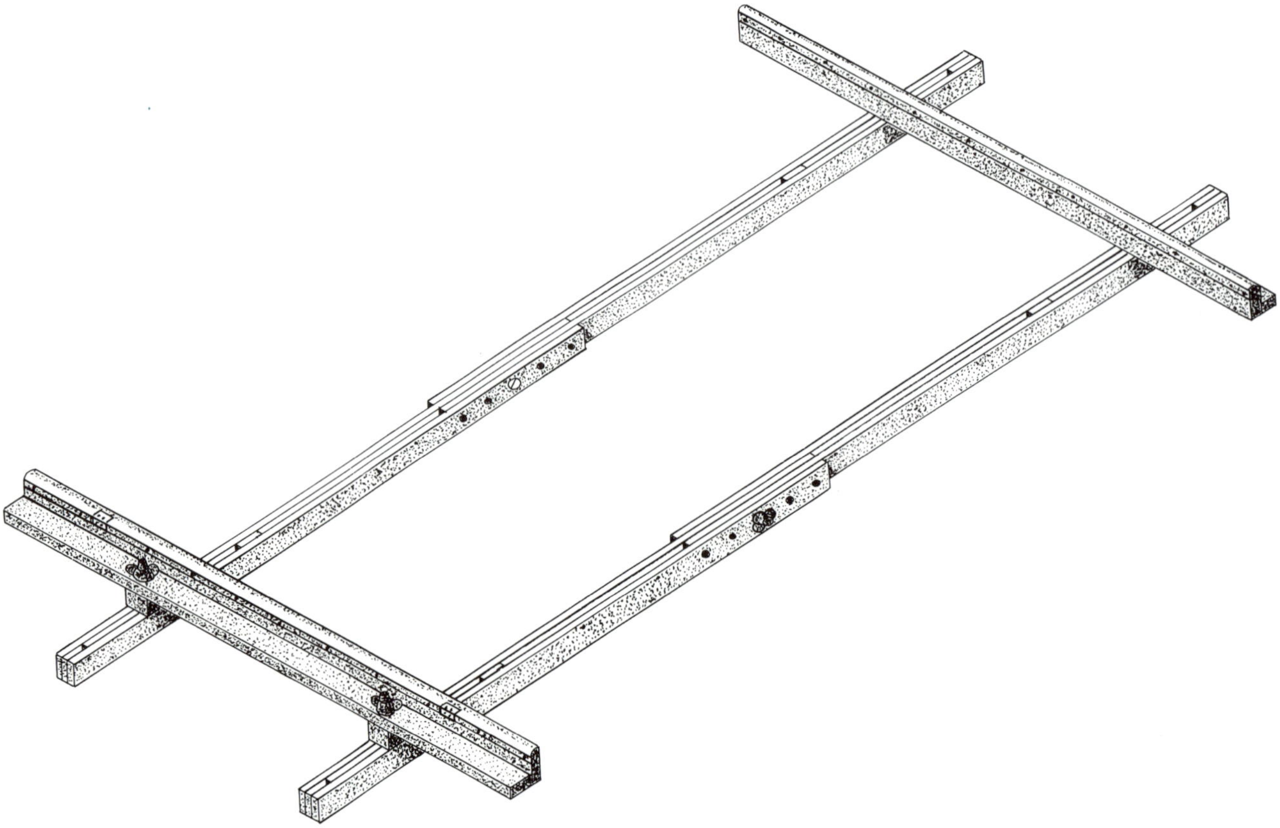

Adjustable wooden slot frame

This softwood frame has slots cut at intervals down each side enabling you to adjust it for differently sized squares and rectangles.

It is essential to stretch the silk evenly and tautly. I suggest you protect the frame with masking tape first. The ideal pins to use have three small points to hold the silk firmly, and they can be removed easily. Begin pinning along one side about every 3 cm. Continue along the adjacent side, then stretch the silk taut and pin to the remaining two sides. The silk should be as tight as a drum.

Fixed wooden frame

This can be four pieces of wood fixed together, or an embroidery hoop or an old picture frame will do. The main disadvantage with this frame, however, is that its size cannot be adjusted.

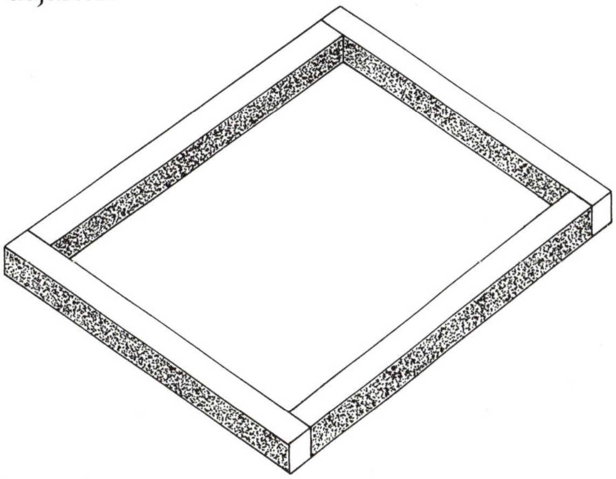

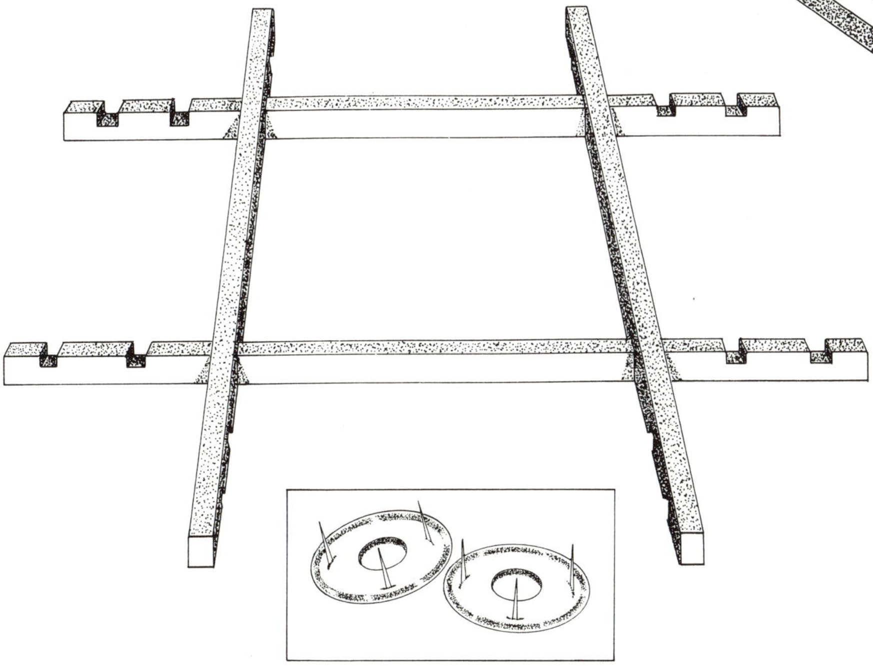

Brushes

Several types of brushes are suitable for silk painting. Different thicknesses are needed for different purposes. Initially I suggest you invest in three – fine, medium and large – and a packet of cotton buds.

It is a good investment to buy the best-quality brushes you can afford, as not only will they be an enjoyable tool to use but, if looked after, will also last you for years. Watercolour brushes with fine points are most useful, as they spring back into shape after each brush stroke and, depending on their size, hold enough dye to cover an area smoothly. I recommend sable brushes, but ox hair, squirrel hair and some cheaper bamboo brushes are acceptable. Remember the lower the number on the brush, the finer the brush.

Spreaders – small, medium and large – are available for painting large background areas quickly and easily. Made of foam and with a wooden handle, they are relatively cheap. Cotton buds are good for beginners or larger groups as a cheap alternative. They are useful for mopping up excess dye too. For large background areas a firm cotton-wool ball wound around a cotton bud or stuck on a peg can be used, but be aware of the fact that it will soak up a lot of dye, so is uneconomical.

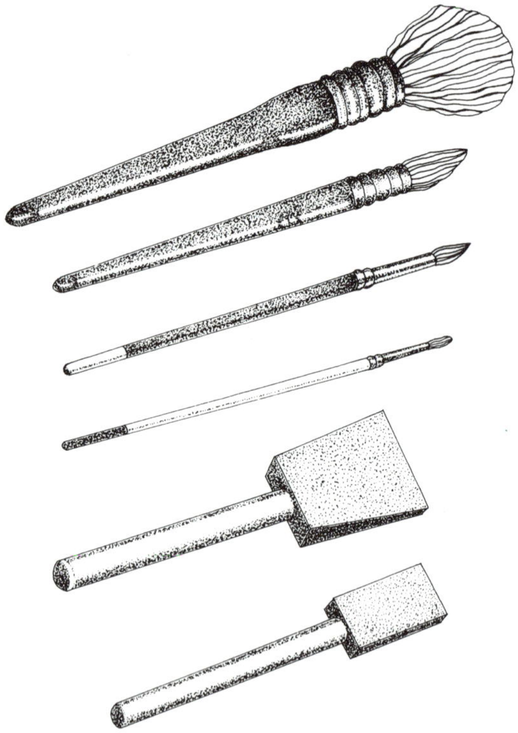

A selection of brushes and spreaders.

Care of brushes

Take care of your brushes and they will last you well. After use, rinse them thoroughly to remove all the dye, especially near the base. With thicker brushes you might use soapy water to clean them. Rinse well, reshape and leave to dry suspended or with the bristles uppermost so that the tips cannot be damaged. Never leave brushes standing in water or sealed away.

Gutta

Gutta is a latex-based substance or a water-based wax that acts as both a design tool and as a resist to the dye. Sold under the names gutta or serti, it contains the sap of the gutta percha tree, a type of rubber tree from South-east Asia. The gutta works by penetrating the silk so that when dye is applied the colour travels along the fabric until it meets the gutta line and stops. The gutta thus allows you to control the designs.

Gutta is usually applied to the fabric with a pipette and a fine metal nib.

For further details, see the section on Gutta on pages 40 to 44.

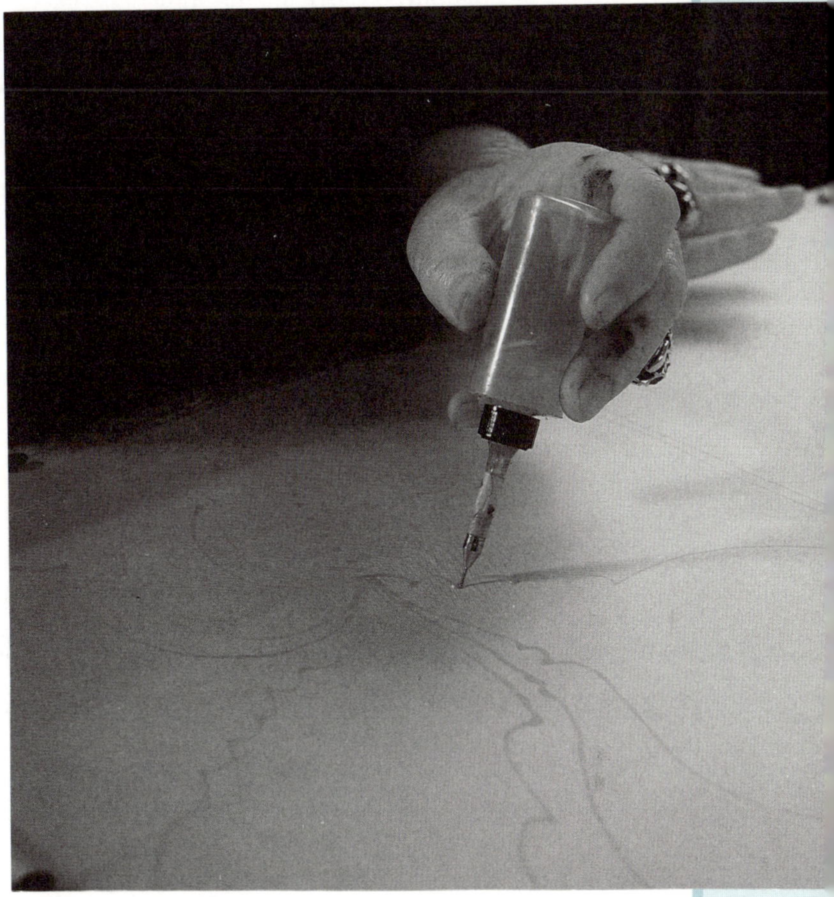

Applying gutta to a design.

Coloured and metallic guttas

There are times when you will want to use coloured or metallic guttas in your work, and you will see in the examples in this book that they have sometimes been used to highlight a design. These guttas are also available in water-based or latex-based form. You can also colour your latex-based clear gutta by using small drops of stained glass colour or typographic ink. Shake the mixture thoroughly before you use it. Water-based gutta can be coloured with drops of dye, but the colour does tend to wash out.

Coloured or metallic guttas should not be dry-cleaned as the chemicals used will dissolve the colour.

While gold and silver gutta are very effective to embellish designs, they do have a tendency to wash off with constant washing. Since this problem has not yet been satisfactorily resolved, they are more suitable for pictures than for clothing.

Pipette and nibs

Pipettes are used to paint the gutta onto the surface of the fabric. The pipette is made of plastic and has a small metal nib attached to it. By applying light pressure to the pipette, the gutta flows out, through the thin slot in the nib, allowing you to draw a fine outline or design onto the silk.

Nibs come in sizes 5, 6, 7 and 8, but I recommend size 7 for most purposes. The pressure of your finger on the bottle and the speed with which you work will determine the width of your gutta lines.

The nibs come supplied with a fine wire, which is useful to unblock the hole of the pipette. Nibs can also be cleaned by soaking them in a thinning agent such as shellite.

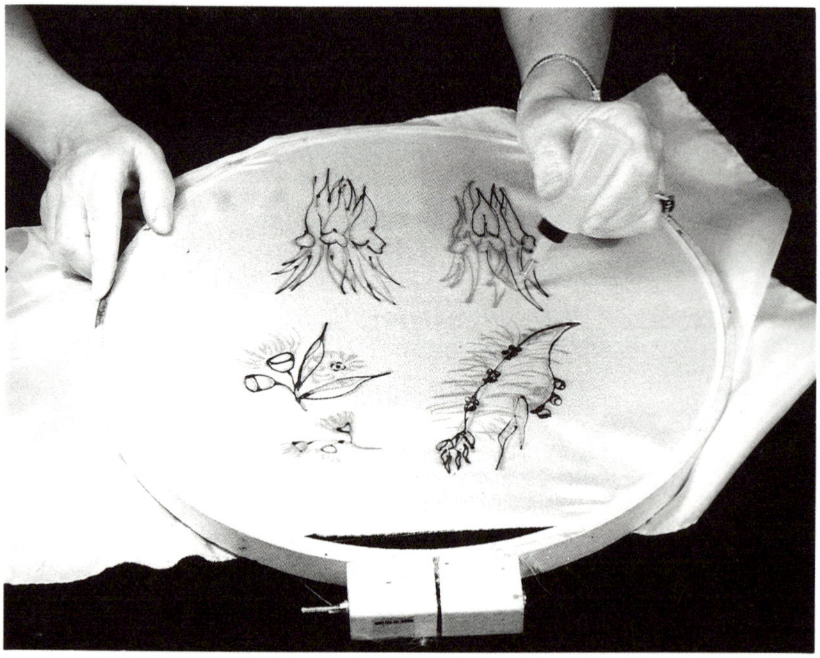

With the fabric stretched on a hoop frame, gutta is applied with a pipette and nib to outline the design.

Wax

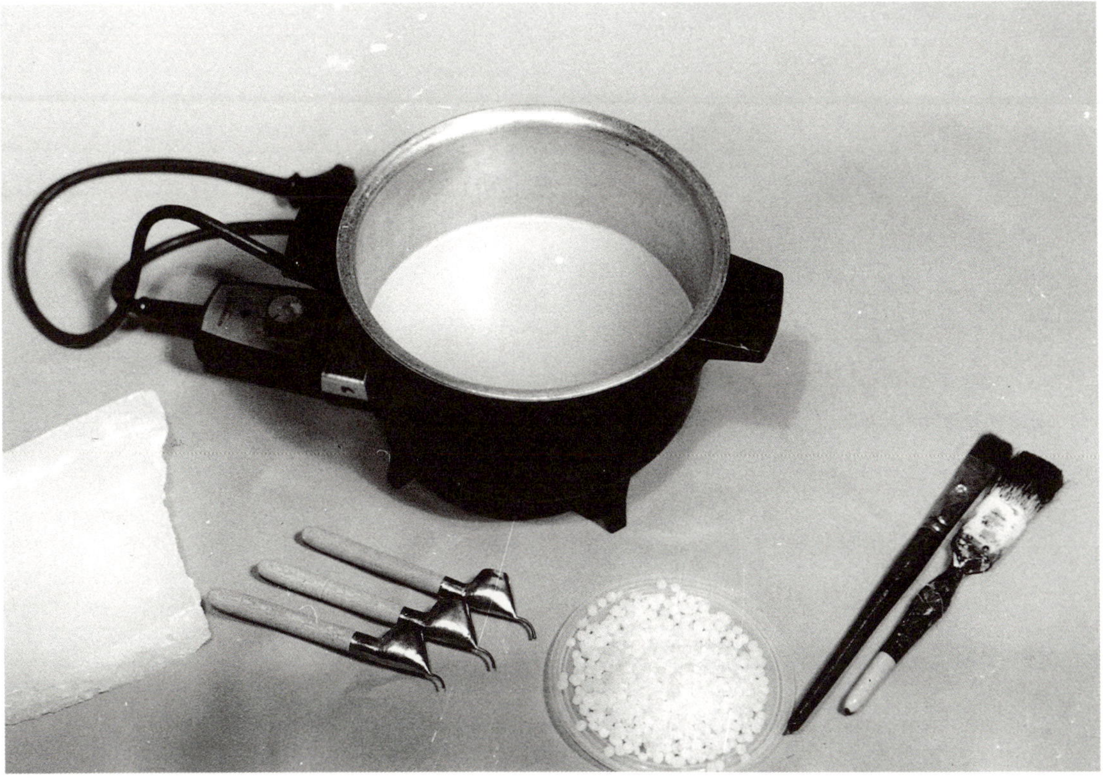

Wax pot and wax, with tjantings and brushes used to apply the wax.

Paraffin wax and beeswax can be used together as a resist for silk paintings instead of gutta. It is used in traditional batik, when the hot wax is applied to the silk so that it creates a barrier by penetrating the fibres, and the waxed area remains undyed.

Paraffin wax is white and comes in the form of candles or blocks. Beeswax is more expensive and is yellow in colour. Paraffin wax can be used alone, but it is very brittle and has a tendency to crack off the silk. The addition of some beeswax helps prevent the cracking. I recommend you use one part beeswax to four parts paraffin wax, but do experiment. The greater proportion of paraffin wax, the heavier the crackle; the more beeswax, the smoother the wax area will be.

For more details on this technique, see the section on Batik on pages 55 to 58.

SECTION 2

Colour and Design

Where do dyes come from?

The history of the dyes used for colour is a fascinating one. Until the 1850s all the peoples of the world – Phoenicians, Greeks, Romans, Peruvians, the known world – looked to nature for the source of dyes for colouring cloth and bark. Blue was obtained for hundreds of years from the indigofera plant, red from the cochineal beetle and the madder plant, purple from the purpura mollusc found on the shores of the eastern Mediterranean. It was so difficult to obtain this creature and so many molluscs were needed to give a strong purple colour that the shade was reserved for the nobility, hence 'royal purple'.

Most plants will produce some dye. Roots, bark, leaves, flowers and berries all yield colours.

It was fascinating for me to learn that almost the complete colour spectrum is obtainable from Australian native eucalypts, acacias, grevilleas, banksias and so on. At the time of European settlement in Australia in 1788, chemical dyes were already widely used. When Australian Aboriginal people wanted colour for paintings or to decorate the body, they used earth pigments, not the colours from plant roots or bark.

Leaves, stems, roots, bark and flowers can be used to produce dye colour.

Using colour

The landscape is a continuing source of inspiration. Here the soft mountain mists and the outline of trees form an intriguing pattern.

Of all the design elements, colour is probably the most appealing and the most exciting. It has been called the 'music of the visual arts'. Like the basic notes in music, colour has a myriad variations and a capacity to affect people emotionally; therefore, colour and music both have a universal ability to express every subtle mood, emotion and intellectual or visual experience.

It is the Australian landscape that inspires my use of colours in fabric: the intense blue of the sky, the particular greens of the country-side and the gum trees, the rich reds and yellow of the earth, the greys, whites and browns of the tree barks, the sparkling green of the mountain ferns, the subtle colours of our unique wildflowers. Everywhere there is bold colour and bright light. Experiencing and photographing all this beauty is a joy, and it heightens my visual awareness and stimulates my desire to translate it into fabric for clothing and pictures.

Colour and light

'Colour is life, for a world without colours appears to us as dead', wrote Johannes Itten, who is considered to be one of the greatest teachers of the art of colour.

Objects we identify as red, yellow or blue are not innately those colours. Rather, we perceive them as being red, yellow or blue because of the way the light strikes them and the message our eyes transmit to the brain.

The science of colour is a complex one. We know colour is actually produced by light. In 1676 Sir Isaac Newton, using a triangular prism, discovered that sunlight (white light) consists of a spectrum of colours: violet, indigo, blue, green, yellow, orange and red. He then had the idea of joining the colours into a circle so that the flow of tone to tone would be continuous. He established that colour is basically sunlight, and that all colours of the spectrum together form white light. When an object reflects all the colours of the spectrum it appears as white. When light is totally absorbed by a surface, the result is black. If an object absorbs all but, say, the red wavelengths of light, and reflects the red, the object appears red.

Many factors influence the way in which light is absorbed or reflected. The bush in sunlight, for example, displays great colour variations depending on whether you see leaves in sunlight or in shade. Some of the most dramatic colours in nature are directly associated with light – the vivid red of a sunset, the bush in flower after rains, the russet tones of autumn.

The Impressionist painters exploited this effect to the highest degree. They tried to paint what we actually see. That is, they tried to see forms in terms of shimmering light and colour, breaking up visual images into tiny dabs of coloured paint. Textile artists can relate to Impressionism: we use repetitive patterns created by weaves, stitches or decoration on fabric.

Colour theory

Many scientists tried to explain the theory of colour in terms of a colour wheel. Johannes Itten developed the twelve-hue colour wheel from the primary colours (red, yellow, blue) and the secondary colours (orange, green, violet) with the tertiary colours, the subtle shadings that are a blend of a primary with a secondary colour. The sequence of the colours is that of the rainbow or natural spectrum.

Colour properties

Colour is generally defined as having three properties: hue, value and intensity.

- **Hue** is the name by which we identify a colour, such as red, blue, orange.
- **Value** refers to the relative lightness or darkness of a colour.
- **Intensity**, also known as 'chroma' or 'saturation', describes the relative purity of a colour. Intensity is dependent upon hue.

High Flyer by Ellie England.

Rainbow Oz by Colleen Weste (see page 53 for a detailed description).

Colour wheel

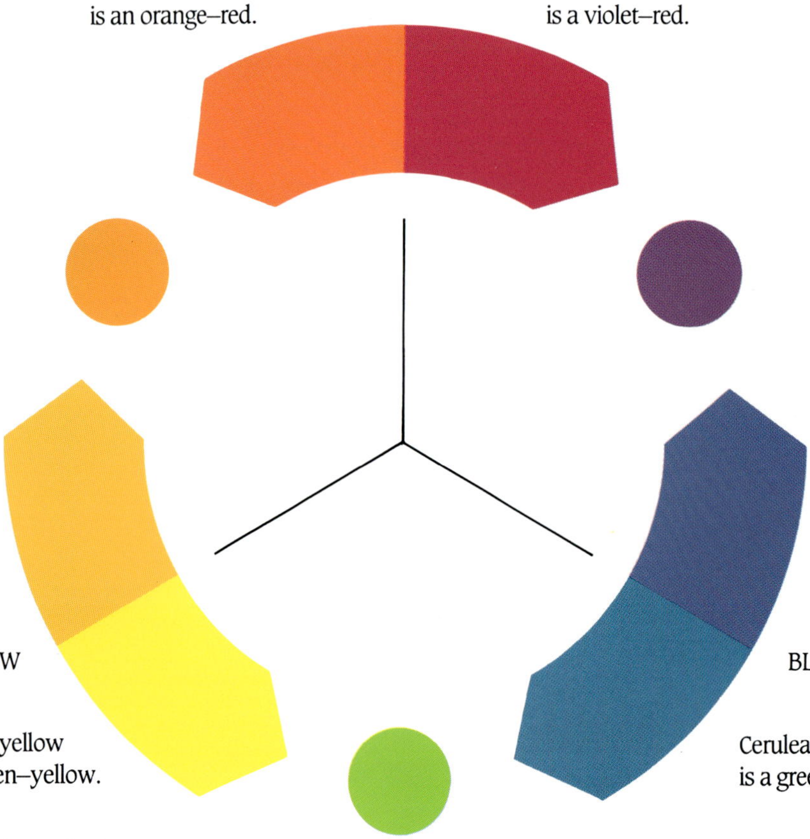

Colour bias wheel

Colour harmonies

When referring to relationships in the colour wheel or when using two or more colours together in a design, we talk about 'colour harmonies'.

- **Monochromatic harmonies** are based on the use of one colour with light or dark variations.
- **Analagous harmonies** join colours that are adjacent on the colour wheel such as blue, blue–green and green.
- **Triad harmonies** are three colours equidistant on the colour wheel, such as orange, green and violet.

Artists have used these systems for centuries.

Colour mixing

For many years students have been told they could mix all of their colours from the three primaries: red, yellow and blue. This is true to a point, but which red, which yellow and which blue? The palette is too limiting and what represents pure red, yellow or blue? In fact, you need two reds, two yellows and two blues to get the full range of colour combinations.

Michael Wilcox in his book *Blue and Yellow Don't Make Green* explains the limitations of the three primaries system and replaces the traditional colour wheel with the 'colour bias wheel'. The six colours in this wheel are an orange–red, a violet–red, a green–yellow, an orange–yellow, a violet–blue and a green–blue. As the name implies, each of the colour types leans, or is biased, towards a secondary colour.

From this simple system we can then mix a range of greens by using lemon yellow in varying quantities with cerulean blue, and a different range of greens using cadmium yellow and ultramarine blue. Yet another range of soft and subdued greens result from a lemon yellow and ultramarine blue combination. When you mix an orange–yellow and a violet–blue, you will get a dull green.

When mixing purple, a violet–red and a violet–blue will produce a good, clear violet, whereas an orange–red and a green–blue will produce a rather dull, and slightly violet tinted, grey.

Similarly, a red that leans towards violet (alizarin crimson), and a lemon yellow will give a subdued orange, just as an orange–red and a lemon yellow will make a dull, greyish orange. The purest orange mix is made up from a warm cadmium yellow and a similarly warm cadmium red.

Once we are thinking clearly about the way in which colours are biased then we can mix clear, bright colour combinations or subtle, subdued ones. For example a blue that leans towards violet will dull or neutralise an otherwise bright green. If you want clear bright violets, oranges or greens, make them from colours that carry the same bias.

The two colours opposite each other on the colour wheel are called 'complementary'.

To neutralise or subdue any colour add its complementary colour; for example, add red to green, violet to yellow, etc.

Colour contrasts

Any exploration of colour must involve a study of colour contrasts. Let us look at some ways in which you might select themes for your work using one or more of these colour contrasts.

Contrasts of hue Red, yellow and blue are the extreme contrasts of hue. This use of colour is found in folk art throughout the world, and in early stained glass. Matisse, Picasso, Kandinsky and Miro frequently painted using these colours to express simplicity, cosmic universality, joviality, sometimes even profound grief.

Notice in the examples of silk art how the artists have used colours of great luminosity, and especially how, in the piece entitled *High Flyer* opposite page 20, the feathers contrast in hue with black as a powerful element of the colour composition.

Light–dark contrast Just as red, yellow and blue represent the extreme contrasts of hue, so black and white are the extremes of light and dark. The best way to understand light–dark contrast is to study the grey scale. If we break the grey scale down to about nine steps from white to black, we see how value alone can be used to achieve subtleties of mood and effect. The black-and-white photographer uses this as an essential tool, exploring the full tonal range from black through middle values of grey to white to achieve effects. The photograph of the sawmill opposite is essentially a study of light–dark value. The composition succeeds because of the contrasts in value. The dark and light areas reach out to the middle values and create a sense of balance.

The grey scale: nine tones from white to black.

A study in light–dark contrast shows how graduations of the same shade can be used in designing.

Following the grey scale, we can then translate value graduations into any hue. Every hue has a range of values in opposite directions from the pure hue, which is usually considered the middle value. On one side are tints, lighter in value by the addition of white; while on the other side shades are darker in value made by adding black. It is important to notice that the light–dark values of different hues will vary drastically. Yellow, for example, has a pure hue much lighter in value than the pure hue of blue. There is no such thing as a dark pure yellow. Additions of black to yellow make olive green and brown. Pure blue is very dark; light blues are pale and dim. Each admixture of black or white reduces the vividness of a hue, and you must allow for this. Using colours of equal lightness or darkness is a useful resource in any design, because the colours will relate to each other. Hues of equal brilliance using two, three or four tones can give order, clarity and vigour to a composition (see photograph of *Parrots and Waratahs* on page 43 and facing page 5).

Cold–warm contrast The colour spectrum expresses a range of moods. Red, for example, is a colour we associate with danger. It is the most dominant colour in the spectrum. Orange and yellow are less threatening and their warm qualities create an inviting atmosphere, like the amber glow of a log fire for example. The cooler colours of violet and indigo have a sombre, subdued quality, while the cool colours of green and blue evoke a restful, calm response. This expressive feeling of cold–warm contrasts can be used for pictorial effect. In a landscape more distant objects seem to be colder because of 'the air between'.

The artist Monet spent a lifetime painting landscapes, making intensive studies of light and mood changing with the seasons, the time of day and the weather. His clouds and mist, flowing water, and so on depict cold and warm elements rather than simply light and dark variations.

Complementary contrast As already mentioned, colours opposite each other are called 'complementary'. When placed side by side on the colour wheel, complementaries tend to intensify each other, an effect called 'simultaneous contrast'. In nature we see many examples of complementary contrast. Remember flowers are rarely seen in isolation, but rather they are viewed in relation to their surroundings, and very often the flower is the complement of its background, which in turn intensifies the beauty of the flower. One example is the red of the callistemon, or bottlebrush, against the tree's green leaves.

Contrast of saturation This refers to the contrast between pure, intense colours and the more muted, diluted colours. We use the term 'saturated' to describe a colour that is at its most intense and fully saturated with either pigment or light. Both the light and dark values of any colour will have low intensity: the middle values will have high intensity.

By mixing a pure colour with grey or black, you will get less intense and duller colours.

The rainforest theme is captured by varying elements: contrasts in the shape and size of the leaves, repeating flower motifs, large and small rocks, trees and fungi.

Black tends to deprive colours of their quality of liveliness, eventually deadening them. I dislike the effect grey has on a painting and avoid it as much as possible.

Pure colours can also be diluted by the admixture of their complementary colour. Green and red mixed together become grey–black. Diluting colour with grey or its complement tends to neutralise the composition. A colour can also be diluted with white, which will make it appear a little colder.

Variety and unity We have seen from the photograph of the sawmill on page 23 just how contrasts in value can contribute to the success of a piece. They give variety to the picture, and this is necessary in all designs.

In addition, however, there must be a unifying element to control the composition. The ideal is a balance between variety and unity. There are ways in which you can effectively introduce both of these.

Some techniques for creating unity are

repetition of design elements, harmony of colour and an enclosing border. A motif, shape, pattern or size can be repeated through a design. In *White Wildflowers* on page 57 there is a repetition of various wildflowers, each interesting and slightly different. The design is enclosed in black, which gives a unity to the whole composition. The satin cape on page 42 and facing page 68 has a similar variety of gutta shapes and themes. Here the repetition of shapes and patterns provide a form of unity, but the success of the piece is the wonderful blend of harmonious colours to enhance and emphasise the main theme.

Again, in *Environmental Piece, Sale* on page 58 and facing page 53, the artist introduces a great variety of shapes and themes, yet she uses texture and harmonious colours in the landscape to bring a unity to the whole picture. Nature is constantly changing – flowers, rocks, animals – therefore, it provides a treasure house of material from which to explore the play of light and dark, large and small, rough and smooth. Variety is almost synonymous with contrast.

Expansion of colour

One of the special qualities of silk painting is the intriguing possibility for obtaining iridescence, lustre and transparency of colour. Luminous effects can be achieved on silk, giving the effect of the glow of light. You can exploit the play of light and colour on the surface. Using the lustrous silk and transparent dyes, it is possible to create an iridescent effect to capture the effect of a dragonfly's wings in sunlight or the shimmering glow of opals (see *Opal Patterns* on page 47 and opposite the title page). Transparent silk dyes will suggest depth by nature of their transparency. In fact you can easily imply a sense of distance through the use of these dyes (see *Blue Landscape* on page 52 and the facing page). Finally you can add lustre, shine or brilliance with the addition of gold or pearlised gutta or paint.

We have seen that colour can be a most wonderful tool – beguiling, compelling and a lifetime pursuit. You will discover your own way of painting with colour. I have noticed that students intuitively paint best with the colours they prefer and according to their personality type and their 'aura'.

There are no good or bad colours, rather there are just good combinations and bad combinations. Johannes Itten, speaking of colour, is reported to have said: 'If you unknowingly are able to create masterpieces in colour, then unknowledge is your way. But if you are unable to create masterpieces out of your knowledge, then you ought to look for knowledge.' He also said: 'The painter uses forms and colours to project an idea. However painting may evolve, colour will remain its prime material.'

Sources of inspiration

Design is all around you. Just look and you will see colour, shapes textures, forms everywhere. All you need to do is to develop your 'seeing' eye – to really look and absorb the visual patterns around you with a new awareness. Take time to observe them, first noticing the overall shapes and colours, then focusing on the thing that arouses your interest for whatever reason: it may be the way the light falls on a tree silhouetted against the evening sky, some newly shorn lambs whose whiteness contrasts dramatically with the gentle, grassy green hills, or the bright red of gum blossoms in full bloom.

You may want to capture the scene. Some people choose to sketch with pencil or pastels, others record it with a photograph, while others commit the scene to memory to draw on later. Whichever way you choose, by truly noticing your particular environment and

The dramatic pattern formed by the silhouette of a tree against the sky is a good basis for a design to be transferred onto silk.

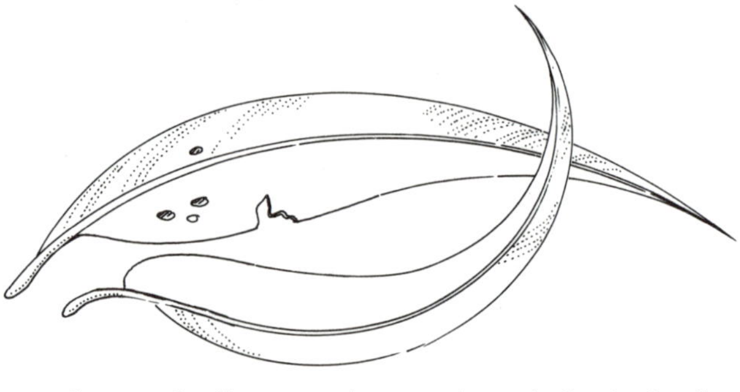

A photograph of leaves on the ground was the inspiration for this sketch. This sketch could then be translated into a silk painting.

absorbing the world of nature, you are storing up in your subconscious a treasure house of design ideas. When you are looking for inspiration it is all there, waiting for you to draw on.

We all interpret what we see in our own personal way. A tutor once said, 'I cannot teach you how to design, I can only lead you into a visual experience'. Design is the ability to see those things that surround us and to recall them in our own personal ways. Whether they are good or bad design is a matter of subjective judgement. Design must go hand in hand with technique and function. A well-designed cup, for example, must work well to serve its purpose. Design is a series of decisions about something, but it does not necessarily give all the answers. It is a selection of ideas that will make a design perfect, but the elements cannot be defined as a mathematical equation where two plus two equals four, whereas x colour in y form will not necessarily make a perfect design.

Design is natural and essential to creativity. In order to make something original, be it a table, an aeroplane or a picture, we use our imagination and acquired knowledge and make something that we hope will be pleasing and fulfil its function. A few select artists and craftspeople show extraordinary sensitivity to their materials and for them designing original work seems to be intuitive. They are rare and special. Most artists and craftspeople spend a lifetime learning, training, observing, usually with persistent effort. Professor Clinton

McKenzie once said of his students, 'Very few of them are truly gifted. It seems that it is those who do all of the work, all of the time that eventually get there. No great artist ever painted occasionally, they worked and worked for years.' Turner spent a lifetime trying to capture the grandeur of nature on canvas. Lloyd Rees when in his nineties was still exploring colour and light in the landscape with a passionate vision. So do not be deterred if your initial efforts are disappointing, start afresh and keep on until you get the effect you are after.

So what kind of tools do you need to translate your visual experience into successful fabric pieces? The most immediately noticeable element of design, and the most exciting, is colour, as discussed in the preceding section. Line is another useful tool and is, perhaps, the most fundamental element. Lines delineate every part of our world from the soaring skyscrapers to the delicate veins of a leaf. Line can convey a feeling, an essential quality. In nature we see infinite variety: the undulating line of hills, the flowing lines of a gown, a snail trail, patterns in the shifting sand, the ripples on a pond, majestic trees with their branches reaching up, mountains against the skyline. Continuous lines form patterns or textures. Mosaic tiles create a fascinating study in lines; marbling and calligraphy are about swirling lines. We can create texture in silk painting by using salt or water to depict trees, rocks and pebbles.

Fossilised wood forms an interesting texture and pattern.

Another important element is space and its relation to forms and shapes. One way of deciding how to use shapes in a space is to cut pieces of paper into shapes and move them about until you obtain a pleasing result. The French painter Matisse used this idea with complex cutouts, often shapes abstracted from nature. When illness prevented him from standing at an easel, he painted sheets of paper in various colours, then cut out and pasted them to create striking designs.

Buildings in our cities display the concept of space on a grand scale. Geometric shapes, the circle, the square, the triangle, dominate the constructed environment. To Pythagoras, a mathematician who changed our way of thinking, everything in life was made up of these basic geometric shapes. He taught that they must be used in harmony. For example, if you only use one shape in a skyline, the effect is unbalanced and unsuccessful. The way we perceive shapes has a psychological value.

Sir Isaac Newton later said that a precise picture of the landscape is a pattern-making process, for example, the way a plant grows, the way a flower opens. When forms in nature are magnified many times, we see still an order, a pattern to everything.

Once we see everything about us in terms of colour, shape and line with an underlying rhythm and balance, then we are beginning to analyse what we see. These are the tools of design.

A word about drawing your designs. I have noticed over the years many of my students have few, if any, drawing skills. Not surprising, as textile artists can spend a lifetime expressing themselves in so many mediums – weaving, stitching, embroidery, dyeing, knitting, quilting. They explore colour, texture, line, etc. with threads and fabric without the need to draw images. Like most acquired skills, it is particularly true with drawing, you need to practise a great deal to feel really confident.

I strongly recommend that you take a drawing class. It will help you to develop your seeing eye and heighten your powers of observation. Many artists attend figure drawing classes with a model regularly. The human body has fascinated man for centuries. It is the most challenging and enticing form, like trying to capture the essence of life.

I like the Zen approach to seeing and drawing, which treats it as meditation. This approach was described by Frederick Franck, an extraordinary artist and writer whose drawings abound in museums throughout the world. His method does not require any previous art training. In this discipline you draw with the hand mirroring what the eye perceives, rather than taking the intellectual approach. Say, for example, you attempt to draw a leaf. Instead of analysing the leaf with your thinking, judging brain, you sit quietly, observing, trying to become the leaf. Then, totally concentrating on the leaf, take your

The contrast between dramatic natural shapes (Wave Rock, Western Australia) and the geometric patterns of a city skyline.

pencil and let it flow on the paper. Feel the pencil going around the line, touching the contours. The idea is to just see and let your pencil follow what you see. It will draw itself. Don't worry if your early attempts are not good. As you begin to feel and experience the subject you are looking at, your work will develop its own validity.

Artists seeking to give depth to their work, use the subject matter they see but only in relation to their own inner personal experience. Henri Matisse said: 'In drawing a tree I shan't get free of my emotion by copying the tree faithfully, but only after identifying myself with it. I have to create an object which resembles the tree.'

Every vista you see could present a starting point for your silk painting. But where do you start? 'To paint is not to copy the object slavishly,' said Paul Cezanne, 'it is to grasp the harmony among many relationships'.

How do you see these relationships in your world and begin to translate them? Some ideas may suggest new approaches to colour, different ways of using shape and form, themes best expressed in abstract form. You might take as your theme a shape. It could be a square, a cone, a cube or even a shape from nature, such as a leaf or a bud. Think of all the ways you might paint it. You might repeat it. Paul Klee used to paint variations on a square, masses of them. His works are individual, they create a graceful feeling of light in motion. Matisse used picture cutouts. Josef Albers dedicated years to his Homage to the Square series: The same shape, just with variations in colour. Concentrate on the colours. Think of them maybe as a transparent play of light, each shape in its own space (positive and negative). Now overlap some shapes, try variations in size; paint some high key, others low key. Exploit the theme in as many ways as you can think of.

I frequently choose to paint in an abstract way. Taking ideas from reality, expressing them in an abstract way and using colour as a means of saying what I experienced with nature, as well as expressing my inner self.

Screen-printed design with abstracted ladybird and umbrella motifs.

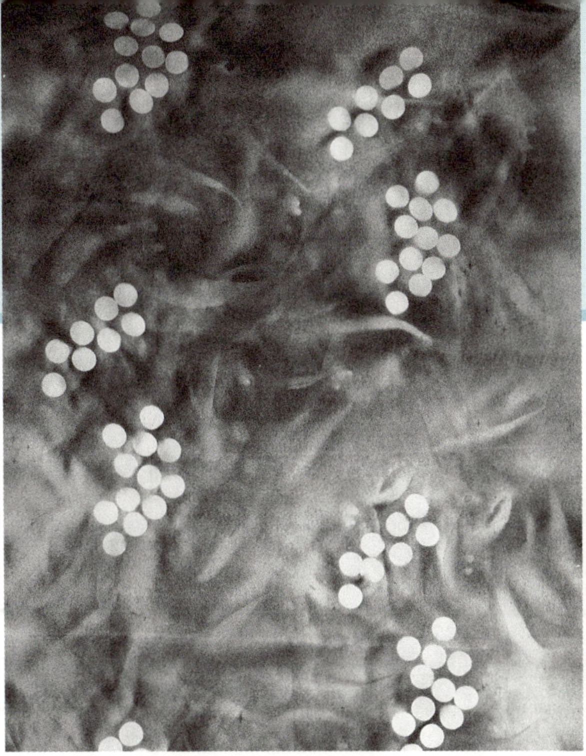

Photograph of wattle blossom with the author's silk painted version of the flowers.

My inspiration, for example, might be rainbow lorikeets. I study the colours, the way they are juxtaposed, the proportion of each colour on the birds, the colour harmonies. Then I paint my fabric purely in abstract shapes, but thinking about how I can convey the idea of the parrots. I try to capture their lyricism and flow, aware of the soft quality of the silk and the way in which it will drape. In an abstraction, you organise colour, shape, movement and balance as you would in any piece. By focusing your attention on design elements other than the subject matter, you become freer and your work more individual.

This process of thinking through an idea, a theme, starts the moment you contemplate painting. Ask yourself three basic questions.

- What do I hope to achieve in the piece?
- How am I going to achieve it?
- What is its end use?

Remember if you are painting some silk for clothing, the fabric is not an end in itself, but you must consider the finished garment. Will the silk be draped near the face as a scarf, for example? Will it be a tailored garment? Will it be a softly draping blouse or skirt? What are the dominant elements – colour, shapes, imagery?

You are beginning to discover your own way. Paint. Paint often. It is only by play and experimentation you discover wonderful things.

Study works in art galleries and museums. Look at how other artists expressed their world. And study your own work. What is your most consistent style? What is most characteristic of you as an artist?

Don't worry if you feel discouraged at times. You are not alone. All artists suffer from it. Discouragement must always be present and faced. Remember accidents to the silk painter (and to any artist) are an interesting learning experience. We are all familiar with them. Out of discouragement progress comes. Sometimes you seem to work and work at something, but cannot get the effect you are after. Then, one day, there is a ray of hope. You discover or create an effect that pleases you and you are soaring on cloud nine. That is when it is all worthwhile – and you are ready to go on to the next challenge!

Photographing nature

Photographing the world around you is creative and challenging. Seeing the world through the eye of a camera also sharpens your visual awareness and is, therefore, an invaluable tool for the artist.

I recommend you take time to walk in the bush, preferably by a river. Sit quietly, absorbing the sounds and sights of the bush. You will notice colour and light, shapes and patterns all around you. Gradually your inner eye will focus on something. It may be the reflections in the clear stream enriched by the varied pebbles that fascinate you. Using your camera lens, your eye becomes more acutely trained to observe colour and light variations in nature. Think about how you might paint with your dyes to capture the beauty of a rippling stream with the sunlight casting reflections all around or the beauty of a wildflower. Store up those moments of seeing and you will have a rich resource of ideas to use.

I always remember the story told by Frederick Franck in *The Awakened Eye* of how his grandfather gave him a stereoptican. 'To this stereoptican I probably owe my way of life', he wrote. This antique gadget consisted

A tree photographed at midday against the vivid blue of the Australian sky.

of twin lens through which he saw an oak tree, for example, not flat as in a picture but in the round, as a living presence. He said that, as a very young boy 'For hours I could sit and watch the miraculous living three dimensionality of cows in a meadow, lovers kissing under a lilac bush . . . round ladies in stays.' For the rest of his life he could see things and people in three dimensions as though he was looking through his grandfather's stereoptican. Realising the potential for his eyes to become 'awakened eyes', Frederick Franck went on to become a unique image maker whose drawings and paintings are collected in scores of museums and whose seeing and drawing meditation workshops are eagerly sought after.

I recommend a pair of binoculars and a macro lens on your camera. They can be your stereoptican.

The modern single lens reflex (SLR) cameras on the market today are virtually foolproof and even a beginner can obtain excellent results with very little knowledge of the theory of photography.

In photography a 35-mm single lens reflex camera is best. Use colour slide film in preference to colour negative, as the latter does not always produce good quality prints. Slide film also gives a three dimensional quality to the picture. A telephoto/wide angle lens from 70 mm to 35 mm with a macro capability will enable you to take wide-angled shots of the landscape or detailed, close-up shots of tiny wildflowers, ladybirds, etc. Looking through

Close-up shots of a Sturt's desert pea and a foxglove taken with a telephoto lens.

your macro lens you will observe many nuances of colour, just as you would through a magnifying glass.

Often you may need to lie flat on your stomach to take a photograph of nature. Rarely can you take good photographs just standing up straight. Remember not to have your shutter speed set lower than 1/60th second when using a hand-held camera, as it will not result in a sharp picture. For good still photography a sturdy tripod is essential. It will result in clear photographs, not those blurred by camera movement. A flash will help control conditions in poor light, for example, you can photograph a flower in the shade on a bush or a dark rainforest scene. The camera can only read for average light so fill-in flash in the dark spots will improve the result.

Filters are a good investment. A UV filter is basic. It cuts down on ultraviolet light and protects your lens from dust and rain. A polariser is excellent in the summer for cutting out the harsh sunlight of our Australian skies. It will also bring up the blues of the sky. We have all seen those scenic photos with washed-out skies. A tobacco filter is useful to bring out the warm and green tones, especially on a dull day.

With nature photography a fascinating world awaits you. Focus on your subject, noting the background. Is it too busy? Does it detract from the subject? Sometimes just by kneeling, squatting or stooping you can solve the problem. With wildflower photography it is best to go in very close, fill your whole frame with one or two flowers only. The depth of focus is very small so background elements are usually blurred while the petals are in sharp focus.

Lighting

This is a vital factor in photographing nature. The ideal times for taking nature photographs are early morning or late afternoon, preferably in sunlight or slightly hazy skies. The sun casts longer shadows from a lower angle at these times of day and thus creates a mood for good photos. The light of the midday sun can often result in a flat effect with little impression of form and texture. The same scene photographed in both the evening and morning light is frequently transformed because the low slanting angle of the sun creates a mood and reveals rich textures and patterns. Often the summer sun at noon in Australia creates very harsh light with intense shadows, thus giving a stark quality whereas when light comes from a lower angle a more pleasing effect is created.

Remember the colour of the light changes during the day as well as the quality. It will be more red in the morning and evening than at midday. An understanding of colour and mood will help you as photographer to produce expressive and atmospheric pictures.

Few photographers can resist a sunset, and to a textile artist they are magical. To capture those soft subtle reds and golden glows on film

Wilpena Pound by Colleen Weste with the photograph (left) taken in South Australia that inspired this piece (see page 48 for a detailed description).

Sunflowers by Robin Rogerson (see page 53 for a detailed description).

A collection of photographs that have inspired the author to try to capture them on silk. Westgate Bridge, Melbourne, at sunset (top left) with the author's interpretation of the scene (top right); detail of wattle blossom (centre left); burning stubble at Yunta, South Australia (centre right); callistemon flower (bottom left); palm fronds (bottom centre); grasses growing in the sand (bottom right).

The dramatic effect of changing light: early morning light strikes a tree; a windmill photographed against the last rays of the sun.

is not so easy. Try not to shoot too early. The photograph of sunset at Yunta, South Australia, (opposite) was taken *after* the sun had gone down.

Film

Many types of excellent film available for the amateur will give a true and full colour range. In my experience 100ASA negative film for prints is a good, general, all-purpose choice.

However, slide film gives you the opportunity to view the enlarged picture through a projector, or it can be made into prints. Slides, unlike prints, also give a three-dimensional view of the subject and are generally required for exhibition or promotion purposes. You can use 35-mm film for your transparencies, although professionals do often use a larger format to obtain detail and clarity. Ask at a good camera shop for further advice on the best kind of film to suit the type of photographs you wish to take.

SECTION 3

Techniques

Gutta

The traditional form of silk painting practised by the French and Japanese is to draw a design on silk using gutta as the drawing tool and design outline; the gutta acts as the resist to the dyes. When applied to the silk, the dyes will travel as far as the gutta line and stop.

Colourless gutta is most frequently used by artists and, in this case, the lines of the gutta remain undyed. However, coloured guttas can be used in place of colourless types or for embellishments to be added after the dye has been applied.

Latex-based or water-based?

The advantage of the latex or rubber-based substance is that, when applied properly, it more consistently resists the dyes than the water-based variety. The water-based gutta may dissolve if too much dye gets near it and the design will be spoilt.

The disadvantage of the latex-based gutta is that it remains sticky, and this stickiness must be removed, after steaming, with shellite, white spirit or by dry-cleaning. This is not necessary with the water-based variety.

The latex-based gutta will go thick eventually if exposed to the air, so ensure the container lid is sealed tightly when the gutta is not is use and do not store gutta in pipettes. If the gutta does become thick and sticky and will not flow freely, thin it down with agent-essence F solvent (diluent for Dupont's gutta) or shellite. Correct consistency of the gutta is vital for good results. If it is too thick, the gutta will sit on the surface of the fabric and not penetrate through the fibres. Conversely, if it is too thin, it will not form a resistant barrier and the dyes will bleed.

Method

1 The sketch of Sturt's desert pea is transferred to the fabric using an erasable pen.

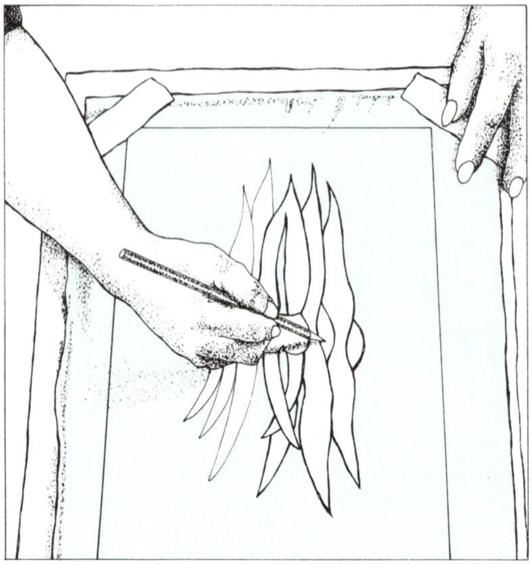

2 Gutta is applied as an outline to the design, using the pipette and nib.

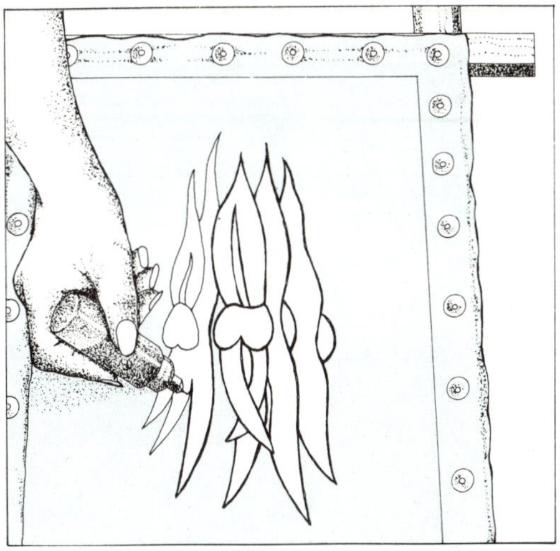

3 The dyes are then applied to the design using a fine paintbrush.

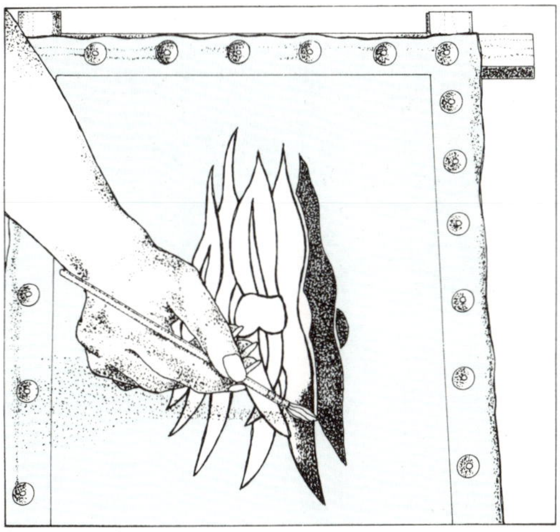

4 The gutta forms part of the design and is not removed after painting. The finished design may be highlighted with coloured guttas.

5 The finished piece is then steam fixed as explained on pages 8–9.

Problems to watch for with gutta

1 Gutta lines do not resist the dyes. This may be because the gutta line is too thin, or you may have drawn the line too fast. Holding the pipette like a pen, squeeze gently to produce an even flow of gutta while travelling slowly over the silk, barely touching the surface. Think of the gutta penetrating the fabric. You should see a transparent line with no breaks in it.

2 The gutta does not penetrate the silk but appears to sit on the surface. The latex gutta may be too thick because of age or exposure to the air. Add a few drops of thinning agent and shake well until a free flowing consistency is obtained.

On the thicker fabric, such as crêpe and wool, the gutta may also need to be applied on the reverse side to ensure it will resist the dye adequately.

3 The dyes bleed through the gutta line. Check there are no gaps in your design lines and, if there are, block them by reapplying the gutta.

The gutta may also not be completely dry. Allow a minimum of 10 to 20 minutes (depending on room temperature) for the gutta to dry. If necessary, use a hair dryer to speed drying.

4 You are using water-based gutta and the dyes are bleeding through. You have applied too much liquid too close to the line, causing the water-based gutta to dissolve. Have less dye on your brush, and paint it on to the fabric away from the line and allow the dye to travel towards the gutta.

5 Dye bleeds through the gutta line or drops on an unwanted area. To remove unwanted dye, place a tissue under the area and rub the spot gently with a cotton bud or brush dipped in diluent and water.

Cape BY THEL MERRY

In this design the gutta was applied first in fine, even lines that penetrated into the silk. The dyes were then applied and then stayed within the gutta area. Clear gutta has been used here. (See colour photograph opposite page 68.)

Pelicans BY LIZ DARBY

Gutta may also be used as a graphic tool. Colourless gutta has been used in this piece to express movement and shape, while clever use has been made of the lines to give a layering effect. The rippling and tumbling movement of the water is created by jagged gutta lines, which are used again in the background to show perspective and give the feeling of distance to the horizon. The pelicans are drawn with great attention to detail, and yet the birds poised in flight have so much movement. (See colour photograph opposite page 4.) Liz Darby's piece *Rosella Flight*, which was painted using similar techniques, appears in colour on the half title page at the front of this book.

Parrots and Waratahs BY JILLIAN TOWNLEY

In this piece clear gutta has been used first to outline the design, then coloured gutta was applied to add interest and fine detail after the dyes blended on the silk. The background, with its strong diagonal lines of colour, contrasts with the bright reds and yellows of the parrots and flowers, while adding vigour and liveliness to the composition. (See colour photograph opposite page 5.)

My Kind of Country BY THEL MERRY

This far north Queensland landscape was painted on silk twill. The artist has captured a feeling of grandeur and wide open spaces, and her choice of vivid colours suggests the heat of the tropical sun. Clear gutta has been applied as a resist first to delineate the landscape. (See colour photograph opposite page 4.)

Salt or alcohol

Salt and alcohol are two of the most popular techniques for a beginner silk painter. Sprinkle the salt on the still-wet dyes, and it is fascinating to watch salt crystals take up the dye and spontaneously create interesting patterns.

Alcohol works in the opposite way to the salt technique. The alcohol disperses the pigment while the salt attracts it. When the alcohol is applied in dots or lines, the dye travels to the outer edges of the silk creating a different, but equally interesting, effect.

Method for using salt

1 The technique with salt is simple. First apply the dyes to the silk and, while they are still damp, sprinkle the salt over the fabric and stand back and wait for the effect. It may take from 2 to 20 minutes for the designs to form. If the weather is hot, you will need to work quickly and apply the salt before the dyes dry on the silk. Therefore, sprinkle salt as you paint, taking care not to use too much salt. If the weather or the salt is damp, heat the salt before use.

2 Undiluted strong dyes produce dramatic textures when salt is applied. By diluting the dyes you will create softer, more flowing effects.

3 Different effects can be produced by using differently sized salt crystals. Rock salt produces large patterns that can be used to depict a rocky coast, minerals or the centre of flowers. Finer salt crystals will produce a grainy effect. Scatter the grains at random or use the salt selectively for effect. If you are using salt only in specific areas, apply the salt technique last if possible, as the salt may accidentally sit on an area where it is not wanted (for example, the border). Take care that no salt gets onto your brush or into the dye bottle, and be careful to keep your work clean.

Salt on wool

Interesting salt effects can be obtained on wool. Sprinkle rock salt on the still-damp dyes (but not too much) and leave for as long as possible. I suggest overnight. Patterns will continue to move slowly for a long time. When

Woollen fabric that has been painted and then sprinkled with salt.

you are happy with the effect, brush the salt off and dry the wool completely before steaming.

Method for using alcohol

1 When using alcohol (methylated spirits are suitable for this technique), paint the dyes onto the background and allow them to dry completely.

2 Using a cotton bud dipped in spirits, dab the alcohol onto the silk for even, round shapes. To paint in fine lines, dip a brush in the spirits, wipe off excess liquid and paint on the silk. This is a useful technique for creating textures such as pebbles, contours, landscapes. You can get similar effects using diluent, which contains alcohol (see the section on watercolour on pages 49–54).

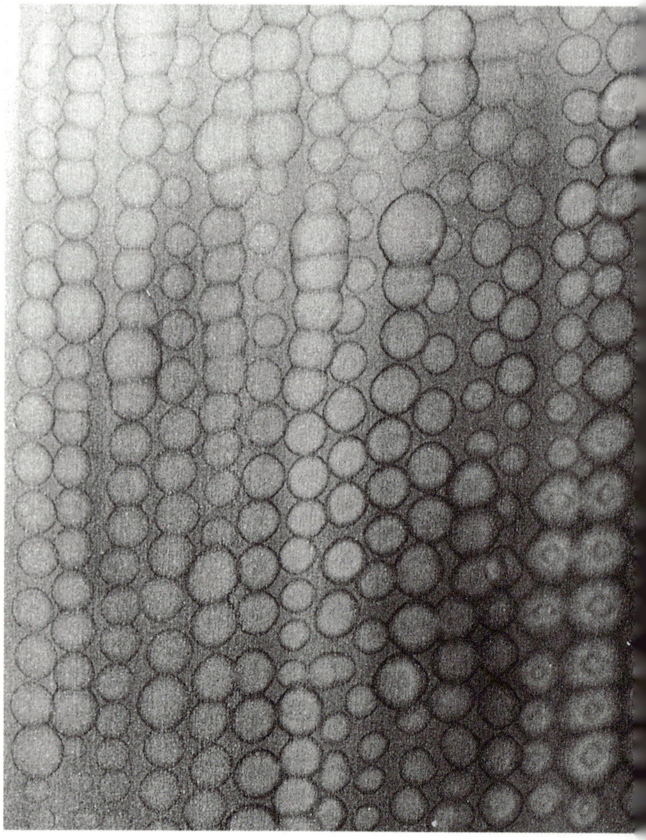

The effect of salt (left) and alcohol (right) on painted silk fabric.

Waratah BY COLLEEN WESTE

Here the flower centres have been sprinkled with salt. The moisture creeps towards the salt carrying colour pigments with it, these accumulate near the salt, to create more intense patches of colours.

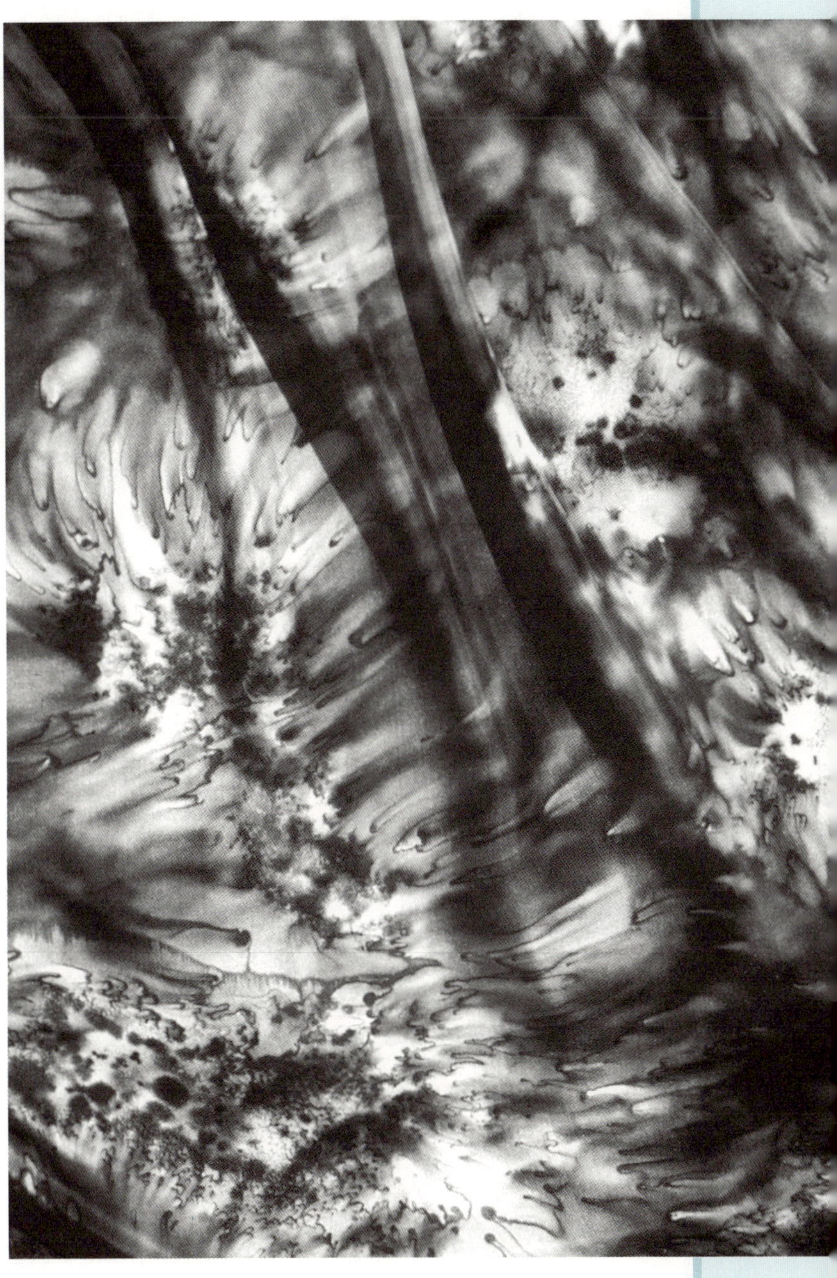

Opal Patterns BY COLLEEN WESTE

This is a favourite salt treatment. Here the dyes are dotted on with very little dye on the brush or sprinkled carefully with a mop brush. While the dyes are still damp, some areas are treated with salt to suggest mineral deposits. (See colour photograph opposite the title page.)

Wilpena Pound BY COLLEEN WESTE

Perhaps you wish to depict a mountain or rocky outcrop, like this one at Wilpena Pound in South Australia. It is seldom satisfying to the creative painter to reproduce a scene as an exact photographic copy. Rather, you can interpret the theme by giving an impression of grandeur and rocky texture.

In this landscape both salt and alcohol effects have been used. Jagged outlines of the rocks and hillsides are created with alcohol, water and salt. Alcohol (methylated spirits) is painted on after the foreground area is dry and a hair dryer is used to stop the process when the desired shapes are achieved. (See colour photograph opposite page 36.)

Watercolour

Painting with watercolours gives the silk painter a great deal of freedom, there are no barriers of gutta or wax to deal with. For me, it is the most exciting and intriguing technique, as I can take advantage of the lustre of the silk and the iridescent effects of the watercolour washes made possible by the transparent quality of the dyes.

This superb medium possesses great fluidity. The artist needs, therefore, to allow the work to flow fast and freely. But you also require discipline before you can take advantage of this freedom. You will need to experiment a great deal to understand the absorbing and reflective qualities of the dyes, to understand the relationships between positive and negative space and to plan successful harmonies. Happy accidents will occur, but sometimes failures do too. Do not worry about failures: you can overdye them at a later date. Most designs are successful because the forms are original and as you keep pushing the colours around freely, your innate sense of composition and colour will take over.

While flowing forms seem to just happen, they will work only when you have a clear idea of the effect you are after. It is also important to be aware of the fabric's end use. For example, the silk for a garment will in many instances be draped as it is worn, so the painting will take on an even richer dimension as the light and shadows pick up the colours.

Method

1 Begin painting by grading colours into and through each other, first on dry silk, then on wet silk. You may find that water marks appear on the dry sample, and you will probably have a stopping and starting line between each colour. Now try to blend the colours into each other by washing between them with clean water to which you have added drops of diluent or diffusing agent.

2 Now wet your next piece of silk all over with a mixture of water and a diluent or diffusing agent (a spray bottle works well for this process). With this wet wash your dyes will now flow freely and water marks should not occur because you are painting wet onto wet. Fill in all the spaces, diffusing the colours into each other. Use the dyes at full saturation or as pastels, but keep washing and blending, always with clean water containing diluent and taking care not to muddy colours. When you are painting in watercolour techniques, you need to find the balance between what the dyes want to do and what you as the artist want to do.

Fabrics

Different effects can be achieved on different types of silk. On fine pongee and habutai, for example, the transparent dyes will travel quickly over the surface, therefore you will have to work faster and use more diluent or water on these fabrics. Using a thicker silk, such as crêpe de Chine, the dyes retain a softer outline and do not spread so fast. It is possible to draw a design with a brush on duppioni, organza or a similar, heavy, fabric and retain the shape of the design.

Diluent

Diluent is also known as 'diffusing agent' and 'wetting agent'. It contains some detergent and alcohol and is, therefore, used with water to dilute the dyes and to wet the silk when painting large background areas.

Diluent will prevent halations, or streakiness, and will help you to achieve an even coloration when painting on silk. It also helps the dyes to diffuse or blend into each other.

It is sold in concentrated form and should be diluted: half a capful in a jar of water. I work with it for all my projects. When diluting the dyes 20 per cent or more for pastel shades, always add several drops of diluent.

Anti-fusant

Anti-fusant is known as 'anti-spread' or 'spreading inhibitor'. When it is painted directly on the silk and allowed to dry, it prevents the dyes from spreading out through the fabric. It is in liquid form and, like diluted gutta, feels quite stiff when dry. It is useful if you wish to paint controlled lines or definite shapes, and it can be applied before or after painting the background. Use it only where you want to stop the spreading of the dye, for example, the outside of a flower, the edge of a border, fine grasses, and so on. You cannot blend colours into each other where anti-fusant has been used. This technique has been used on *Blue Landscape* and *Australian Outback* (both shown on page 52 and on the facing colour page). To remove the stiffness in the silk after using anti-fusant, wash the fabric well after steaming.

Thickener

In order to prevent the dyes spreading fast through the silk, thickener or 'epaississant' may be added to the dyes. An anti-spread solution can be used in proportions from 20/80 up to 50/50 with the dyes. A glue-like thickener is also available from some dye houses, and an alginate called 'manutex' is quite suitable.

Manutex comes in powder form. To make it up, mix 5 g of manutex to a paste with methylated spirits in a screw-top jar. Add 250 ml of cold water. Shake well and leave overnight before using. Pour a small amount of manutex into the dye as required.

Adding thickener to dyes is useful when doing fine, detailed work, like fine grasses, the outline of tree branches or flower petals, or for preventing bleeding in weak gutta areas. It is also used for silk screening (see pages 59–60).

Silk painting using the watercolour technique. Notice that the fabric is stretched on an adjustable pin frame.

Blue Landscape, commission for Minenco Pty Ltd BY COLLEEN WESTE

This is a good example of just how far you can push the watercolour techniques using only two shades of blue. Light and dark areas are achieved by letting the brush flow freely using lots of water and diluent, and creating water marks to emphasise the contours of the landscape. Where necessary, stop the dyes moving by drying them with a hair dryer. Note also the use of anti-spread on the border. (See colour photograph opposite.)

Australian Outback BY COLLEEN WESTE

With this piece, the idea was to suggest the colours and images of Central Australia. Navy borders were applied first over anti-fusant. Wax was chosen as the appropriate medium for graphic lines and circles. Washes of light and dark colours build up the landscape theme and give an impression of distance. Water marks are used to define areas. Finally, the details, such as grasses, were added with a very fine brush dipped in dye. (See colour photograph opposite.)

Blue Landscape, commission for Minenco Pty Ltd, by Colleen Weste (see opposite for a detailed description).

Australian Outback by Colleen Weste (see opposite for a detailed description).

Environmental Piece, Sale by Marie Ingrouille, with a detail of the painting (see page 58 for a detailed description).

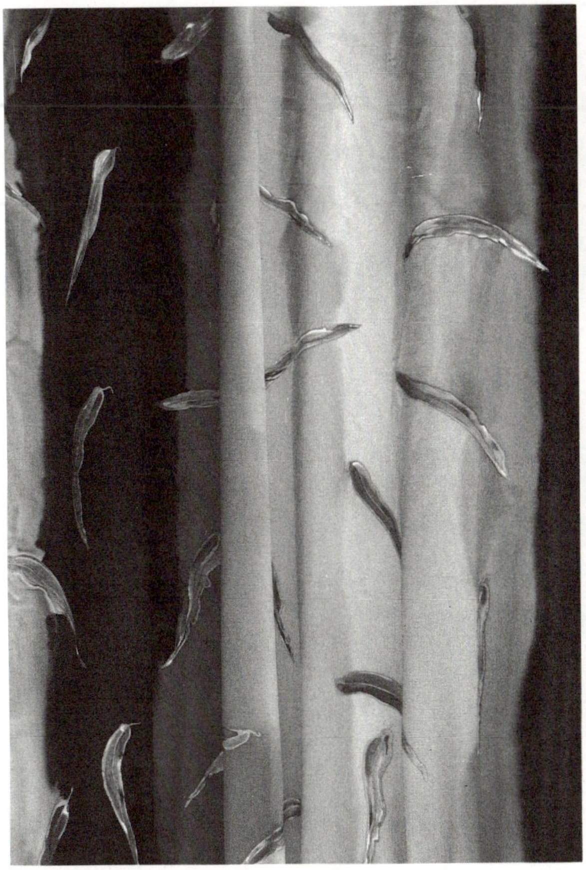

Rainbow Oz BY COLLEEN WESTE

It is important when painting rainbows to merge each colour smoothly and clearly. Speed is essential, and clean water with diluent aids the flow of one colour into another where they join. The gum leaves were painted first. (See colour photograph opposite page 20.)

Sunflowers BY ROBIN ROGERSON

A soft interpretation produced by working with watercolours on a wet silk surface. Controlled designs are applied with a fine-pointed brush containing small amounts of dye. (See colour photograph opposite page 36.)

Fuchsias BY THEL MERRY

This is a dyed and quilted silk Tibetan coat. The design was painted directly onto the silk with no gutta resist to define the areas of colour

Batik

The batik method of decorating fabrics dates back several centuries. In the seventeenth century Dutch navigators brought back from the Orient fabric, paper and leather decorated by means of this technique. The patterns were achieved by wax being applied to the fabric, but without penetrating it. Certain parts of the wax were scraped off in a pattern and the first colour applied to the surface. After this had dried, the first colour was stopped, more wax applied, followed by more scraping and the application of another colour. This obviously was a fairly long process and necessitated detailed preparation of the wax.

Today true batik is still a fairly lengthy process. The design is drawn on with wax using a tjanting, often in very intricate patterns. Then the cloth is immersed in a dyebath. Once dry, the areas that are to remain the first colour are waxed over and the fabric is immersed in a second dyebath. This process may be repeated several times, each overdyeing building up the colours, starting from the lightest and finishing with the darkest, until a rich harmony is produced.

The quicker method that I describe here is known as 'false batik'. The end result may be similar to that of a true batik, but the time involved is less and the use of dyes is much simpler.

Method

1 Heat the wax slowly in a thermostatically controlled wax-pot or stand it in an aluminium tin in water in a saucepan or frying-pan. The wax and its fumes are highly flammable, so work in a ventilated area and take care not to overheat the wax. The wax needs to be kept at a constant temperature of approximately 120°C, so using a thermostatically controlled heater is easier. If the wax is too hot, it will start to smoke, if it is too cold it will sit on the fabric and look white. If applied correctly, it should leave a transparent line on the silk.

2 A tjanting or a small brush is used to apply the hot wax to the stretched fabric. A tjanting is a small copper or brass bowl with a spout attached to a wooden handle. Differently sized spouts create lines of different thicknesses. To use the tjanting, dip the bowl into the hot wax. Leave for a

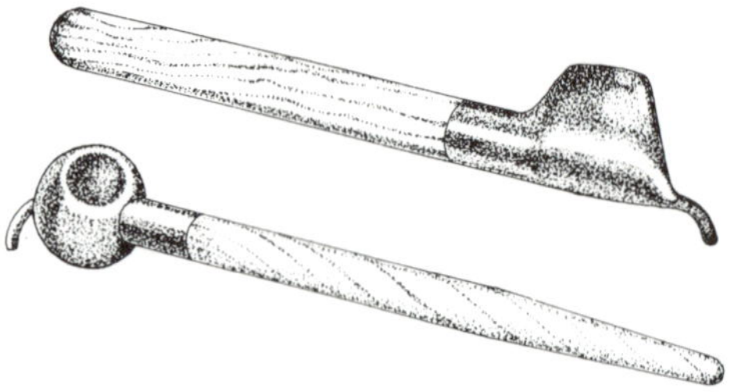

few seconds, then tip up and, using cotton wool or a piece of card to prevent the wax dripping over your silk, transfer the tjanting from pot to fabric.

3 Hold the tjanting in your hand as if you were holding a pen and trail the spout across the silk. Practise making long flowing lines, aiming for even, transparent coverage. Then try small intricate designs, including dots and lace-like squiggles. With practice you will achieve mastery and feel quite relaxed (the wrist action should be loose). Mistakes are hard to remove, so practise on samples until you feel comfortable.

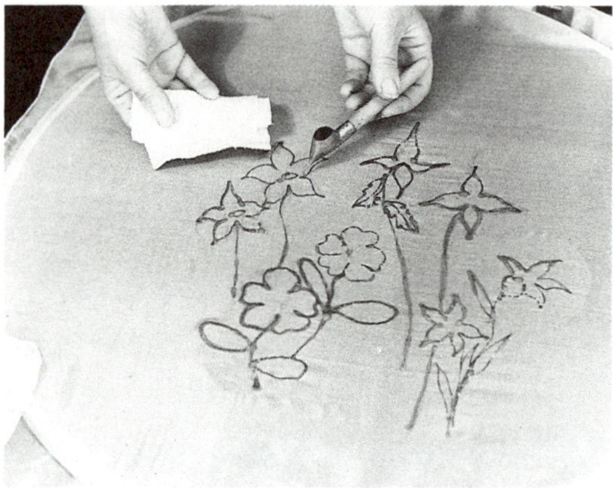

4 Differently sized brushes can be used to create textures and thicker lines. To cover a large, plain area, use a house-painting or flat-headed brush. Interesting textures can be created using a stiff fan or bristle brush and to get a spattered effect you can flick the tip of a bristle brush.

Note: Quality is not important when choosing brushes for applying wax as they tend to have a short life because they are constantly being dipped in melted wax. Short-head bristle brushes are ideal. Wax brushes can be cleaned in white spirit or hot water, but this is difficult. I suggest you set aside brushes to be used solely for wax technique and clean them by just melting the old wax each time in the hot pot.

5 The background areas are then dyed in the same way as for the silk painting technique using gutta.

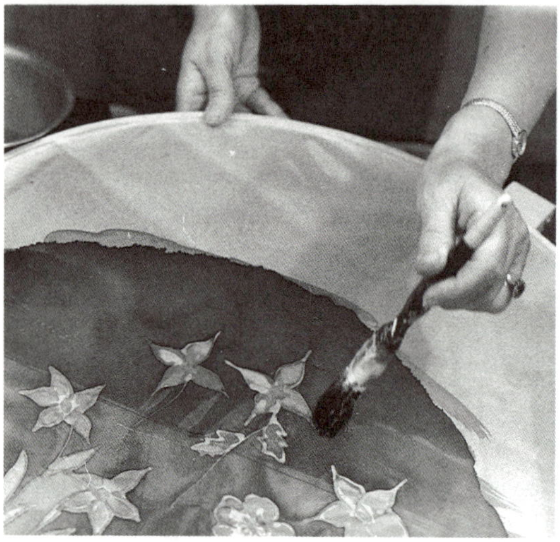

6 To obtain a crackled texture, remove the silk from the frame and crumple it in your hands to crack the wax.

7 Apply dye to the whole surface to penetrate the cracks.

8 The fabric is then placed between several layers of paper, and the wax is removed by ironing it through the layers of paper, which absorb the wax from the fabric.

9 The dyes are finally steam fixed as described on pages 8–9.

White Wildflowers BY COLLEEN WESTE

So that the flowers remain white, they were first waxed using a fine brush. Some of the background design was added with a tjanting. See the illustrations on this page for the step-by-step details of this technique.

Environmental Piece, Sale BY MARIE INGROUILLE

The intention of the artist was to depict the town and environs of Sale in such a way that it would appeal to a young child. In the foreground she depicts the rich rainforests and insects present in the area. The nearby lake and river winding through the town abound with water birds and fish. The main street is lined with notable buildings; the artist has included fine details, such as their stained glass windows. The picture is full of interesting detail that holds the viewer's interest. It flows with life and movement – the train coming into town, animals in the bush, a boy on a bicycle. There is a freshness and liveliness to the whole scene. Techniques used are wax resist, colour blending and salt for texture. (See colour photographs opposite page 53.)

Wildflowers BY MARIE INGROUILLE

In this painting the artist has applied the design with a fine tjanting and heated wax. She has complete control over her tjanting and is able to produce fine delicate lines and dots. The flowers in delicate, blended colours are painted so as to give a lightness to the design. A rich kaleidoscope of colours contrasts with the dark background. (See colour photograph opposite page 68.)

Screen printing and stamping

While I do not usually encourage the use of stencils in my beginner silk painting classes, I believe the method described here is so simple and has so many applications on silk (or any fabric or paper for that matter) that the experienced artist will find innovative ways of using this art form.

Several years ago my feeble attempts at screen printing convinced me that I preferred the freedom of painting the fabric by hand. Not for me the tedious job of cutting stencils and screening repeat designs that required exact registration, etc! Then I was introduced to Print Gocco by Riso. This is an instant, relatively cheap stencil maker and printer.

With the Riso system, making your own stencils is very simple. Basically the design you wish to print can be a clean photocopy or a drawing done with a carbon pen. The prepared design is placed in the pad of the printer, a mesh screen is fitted in place and over the screen window, and a housing containing two bulbs is fixed into position. The lid is pushed down and instant electrical contact is made and the bulbs flash. The screen is now cut and ready to use. The stencil can be used in two ways.

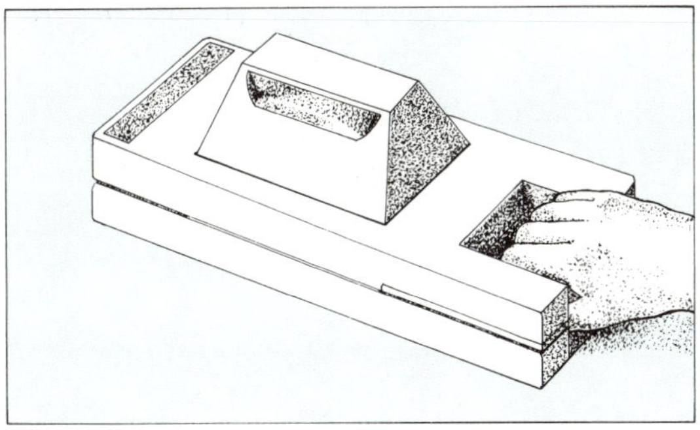

Method for printing or stamping

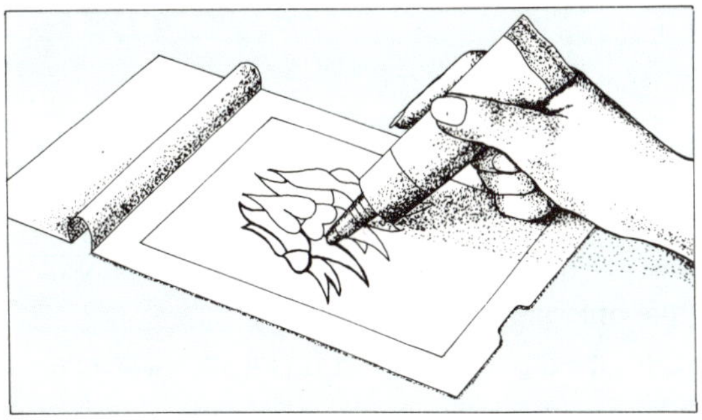

With this method, the stencil is inked up with one of more colours of your choice, placed inside the lid of the printer and the fabric or paper to be printed sits on a small pad. The lid is lowered with one hand, and presses the screen onto the fabric or paper. More than fifty prints may be made before you have to ink the stencil again and the stencil can be used for hundreds of runs.

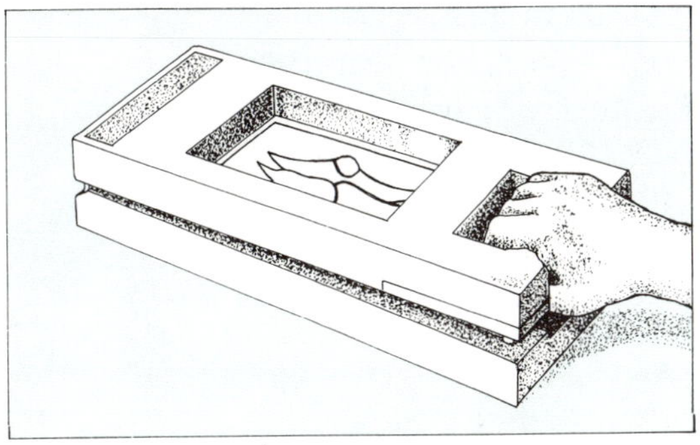

I use this system for all my care labels, business cards, letterheads and scarf prints. For printing multi-coloured designs onto larger pieces of fabric or, for example, on T-shirts there is a separate stamping pad. When doing this, the fabric is held flat by an adhesive board to prevent it from slipping.

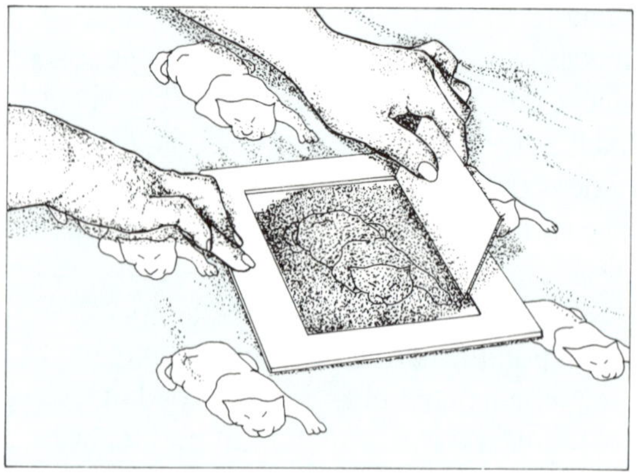

Method for screen printing

To do screen printing use the Riso printer and a wide-mesh screen to cut the stencil – it will take only seconds. Then fix the stencil to a standard-size screen that has a sticky strip to hold the mesh in position. Some ink is put on the master stencil and a print is made by pushing the ink across the stencil with the squeegee.

1 Lay the stencil in place on the fabric.
2 Apply a small amount of black gutta across the top of the screen.
3 Holding the stencil firmly in one hand, grasp the squeegee in the centre with the other hand and, applying a little pressure, push the squeegee down the screen, then up again, in a smooth action.
4 Carefully lift the screen off the fabric.
5 Taking care not to smudge the screened design while it is wet, repeat the procedure again to reproduce the design in different positions.
6 When the gutta is dry (this will take at least 20 minutes), apply the dyes to the design and background. Some details, for example, animal stripes may be added using thickened black dye or textile marking pens.

Airbrushing

The airbrush has a magical quality: it draws and paints without actually touching the surface. It is ideal for graphic imagery and is widely used, therefore, in the advertising industry.

The airbrush was invented in 1893 by Charles Burdick, an unremarkable watercolourist who, nevertheless, gave the art world a unique new tool. Burdick's aim was to develop a mechanical brush capable of laying on a transparent layer of colour more efficiently than the conventional brush.

In the 1920s and 1930s the potential of the airbrush was explored by cubist and surrealist artists such as Kandinsky, Klee and Ernst. It came fully into its own as the Art Deco movement flourished, when it was used for artwork, fashion art, fabric decoration, posters and figurines. Its popularity faded for a while, until the 1940s and 1950s when American car manufacturers used it for glossy car advertising. The airbrush was also ideally suited to the psychedelic art of the 1960s. Its popularity waned again until this decade, when it is now recognised as part of an international art form and is commonly used for animation and effects, ceramics, consumer packaging, retouching photographs in graphic art and, of course, fabric design.

Today's airbrush is a rather more sophisticated precision instrument than the one Burdick made, but the basic principle is the same. An instrument for applying liquid ink or dye, the airbrush has more in common with a pen than with the traditional artist's brush.

Paint is drawn up into the airbrush from a cup-like reservoir and is atomised by a rush of air as it passes through the nozzle, expelling a fine spray of the paint.

Many different types of airbrush are on the market, ranging in complexity and price, and you would be well advised to shop around. Initially you will want to spray fine washes of colour onto fabric or paper.

Types of airbrush

The simplest and cheapest form of atomiser is a mouth diffuser. This consists of a metal tube, which is inserted in a pot of dye then blown through to produce a fine mist. It takes some practice to control the spray well.

Dupont sell an 'ecospray', which is relatively inexpensive. It consists of a pressure spray pack that is attached to a bottle of dye and, when pressed, produces a fine spray. It is non-toxic, non-corrosive and non-flammable. One ecospray lasts 20–35 minutes and sprays about 400 cc of liquid. Replacement cans are available and to change the colour of the dye, simply remove the bottle and refill it.

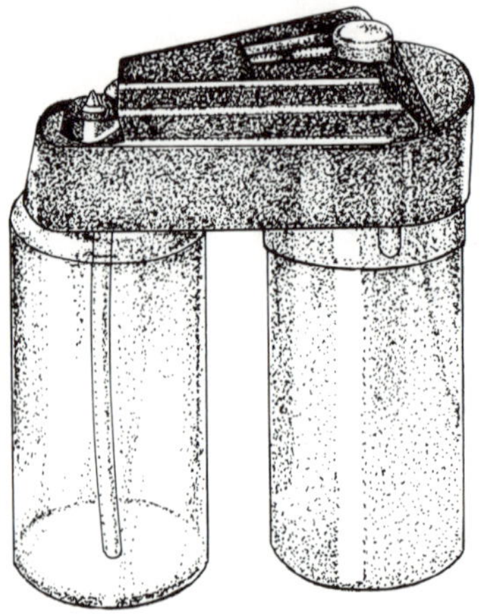

At the other end of the price spectrum is an airbrush – an expensive piece of equipment, but one that is ideal for the purpose. This will give you considerably more control than the ecospray or an atomiser. The airbrush is powered by a compressor or a gas bottle, which is attached to it with a tube.

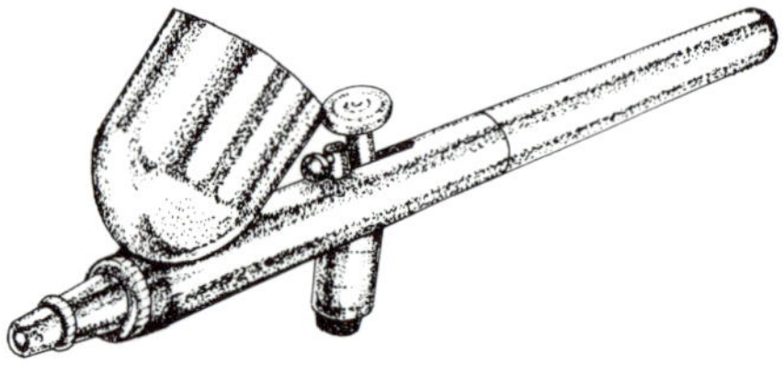

Stencils

When spraying a design onto silk, you may choose to use a stencil. Ready-made stencils are available from specialist shops or you may prefer to make your own. It is best to use pre-treated stencil paper, thick acetate film, heavy paper or card. A sharp cutting tool is needed to cut the stencil design; special cutters with a sharp-pointed blade can be bought from craft shops.

A wooden board or a good, self-healing cutting mat is worth investing in, as cutting will not mark the surface of these.

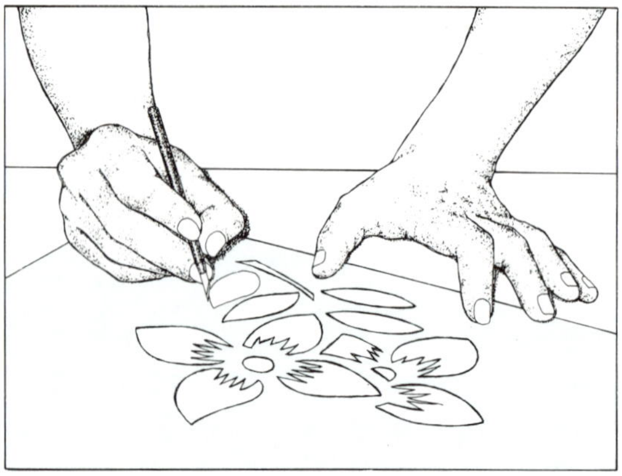

Choosing a design for stencilling

For your first attempts, keep the design simple, as it is difficult to cut intricate patterns.

Stencils can be positive or negative. A positive stencil has the actual shape and design cut away, so after spraying, the masked background will remain undyed and the cut-out shapes will be coloured. A negative stencil has the background cut away. After spraying, the shape will remain undyed and the background will be coloured. Negative stencils can consist of leaves or pressed flowers from nature, which can make most effective designs.

Method

1 When airbrushing with a stencil, it is advisable to treat the silk first with anti-spread. Allow it to dry thoroughly.
2 Attach the stencil with double-sided tape or lay a weight over it (small coins are good).
3 Place a small amount of thickened dye in the first colour in the diffuser. Airbrush the dye onto the silk. Repeat the process several times, waiting for the dye to dry between each spraying. Several coats of a fine spray produce better results than one heavy spray.
4 Experiment by using more than one colour on the same stencil or have different stencils for each colour, for example, one for the leaves and another for the flowers. Interesting effects can be achieved by changing the position of the stencil between sprayings. Try placing the stencil so that it overlaps the earlier image to give different densities of colour.
5 It is important not to overload the fabric with dye. Also, do not hold the air spray too close to the fabric, about 20 cm away is ideal.

Applying paint through a stencil onto silk using an airbrush.

The finished stencil of wildflowers.

Arashi shibori

Shibori is defined as cloth that is given a three-dimensional shape and then dyed. 'Arashi' or 'storm' is the name that the Japanese have given patterns that are resist dyed by wrapping the cloth around a pole, compressing it into folds, and then dyeing it. Many of the traditional patterns suggest rain driven by a strong wind. The design patterns and effects are subtle, but unpredictable. No two pieces of cloth are ever the same. It is precisely the irregularities, like the changing patterns of wind-driven rain, that give these fabrics their special beauty.

There are several adaptations of this process of wrapping fabric around a pole. The traditional methods and patterns formed by wrapping and dyeing are described fully in *Shibori: The Inventive Art of Japanese Shaped Resist Dyeing* by Wada, Rice and Barton. Variations in the patterns depend on the angle at which the cloth is placed on the pole, the surface resists used, the way the fabric is twisted as the folds are compressed, the size of the cylinders and the different thread weights used to tie the fabric. When the fabric is dyed by dipping the pole into an indigo bath, the line patterns and diamond-like forms are strong and dynamic. Different dyeing methods will give a different colour penetration.

I have adapted the process to achieve my own three-dimensional effects that are pleasing. I am searching for a balance between spontaneity and a control over the creative process.

Inspired by the Japanese master Itchiku Kubota and his descriptions of this technique, I continue to experiment with the process, wrapping and rewrapping the silk many times and in different directions, dyeing and over-dyeing with French dyes, or even discharging, until I achieve the effect that I want. Each piece of dyeing gives a fascinating and unpredictable result. Silk is a very tactile medium.

Perhaps the process of shibori has been removed from its traditional context. I see it as an art form, whether it is used for artistic, three-dimensional textile pieces or for garments that are wearable art and make a link between the Japanese feeling for fabrics and their treatment of the kimono as an art form.

Method

1 The silk is fixed around a plumbing pipe with masking tape.

2 Thread (a 20/4 cotton or something similar) is secured with masking tape to the cylinder and is then wound around the fabric. With the cylinder in a vertical position and one end resting on the floor, rotate it with one hand while the other hand controls the tension and placement of the thread. Try to keep a tight tension with the threads as evenly spaced as possible.

3 After winding about 10 cm with the thread, grip the cylinder with both hands and push up the wrapped cloth, compressing it into tight folds.

4 Continue this process step by step until the whole piece is in tightly compressed folds. Secure the thread with tape. The cloth is now ready to be dyed.

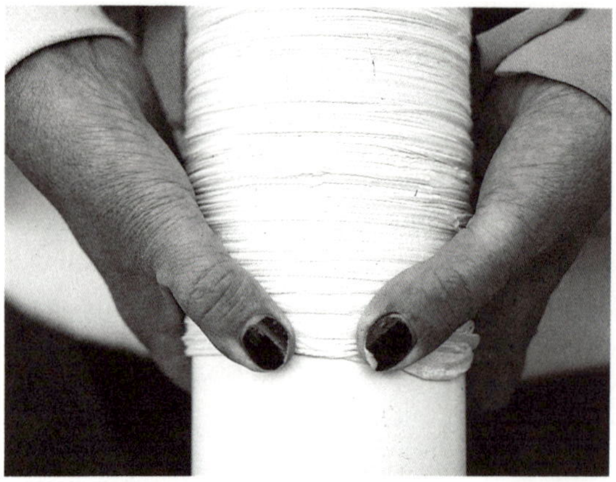

5 Immerse the cylinder in water for several minutes to thoroughly wet the cloth. This is an important step as it swells the winding thread, giving a sharper resist effect, and it also slows the rate of dye penetration.

6 Stand the pole in a tray. Paint the dye onto the cloth with a brush, allowing the colours to blend into each other.

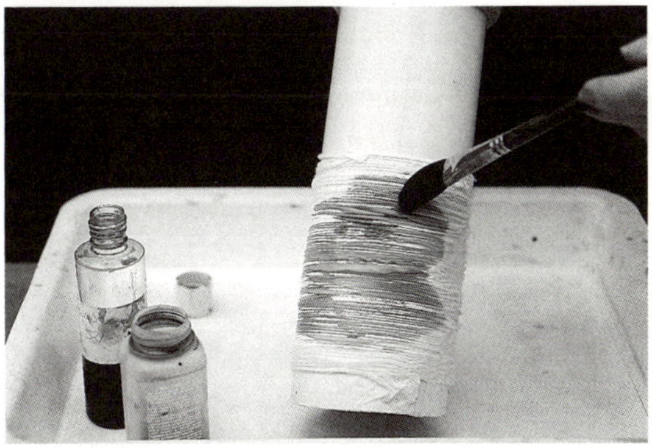

7 Allow the fabric to dry. To fix the dyes, you can use one of two methods. The first is to steam it on the cylinder for 1 hour and 20 minutes. The second is to cover the cloth with a sizing such as spray starch or glue. Allow this to dry, then remove the fabric from the pole disturbing it as little as possible. Then wrap and steam the fabric. Steaming will fix the dyes and hold the pleats in place.

8 Repeat these basic steps two, three or four times, easing out the pleated silk and wrapping each time diagonally in a different direction. Each process changes the design and each application of the dye builds up a richer effect, making the colour more intense.

9 The cloth may be left in its three-dimensional, pleated form or steam-pressed flat with an iron, depending on the use you wish to put it to. The cloth sensitively records the shape and the pressure exerted by the binding thread. It is the 'memory' of the shape that remains that is the essence of shibori.

10 If you wish to retain the pleats, when washing the fabric, do so gently by hand, squeeze out the excess moisture, twist the fabric tightly and allow it to dry completely while twisted.

Butterfly BY COLLEEN WESTE

Habutai silk was tightly wrapped around a cylinder and compressed into folds. Dyes were applied and were allowed to dry. The piece was then steamed on the cylinder. The whole process was repeated three more times. Each time the silk was bound in a different direction and the colours overdyed, then steamed. The result is a rich, fascinating, three-dimensional fabric. (See colour photograph opposite page 68.)

Fawn BY ROSEMARY CHENEY

This porcelain doll is dressed in shibori fabric. The silk was first dyed in woodland colours, then wrapped around a cylinder and overdyed, and finally steamed. The result is a tightly pleated fabric. The dress is shaped by pinning the fabric out to size and steaming it with an iron held above the fabric for a few seconds.

The doll won the Dollmaker of the Year award in 1990.

Cape by Thel Merry (see page 42 for a detailed description).

Butterfly in arashi shibori by Colleen Weste (see page 67 for a detailed description).

Wildflowers by Marie Ingrouille (see page 58 for a detailed description).

Tropical theme for a sarong fabric (page 71).

Dramatic jacket with quilted butterfly motif (page 74).

Camisole and French knickers (page 72) with motif outlined in gutta.

Silk scarf (page 71) painted using the watercolour technique, and brooch with silk painting between layers of perspex (page 73).

SECTION 4

Projects

Sewing silk

When sewing silk on a sewing machine I use a size 70/10 ballpoint needle. Silk is a tough fibre and, therefore, you will need to change your needle often to avoid any blunting of the needle, which will cause pulling of the threads of the fabric.

Use a fine silk thread to machine stitch the edges of a scarf before you dye the fabric. The dyes will then be taken up on the thread as well. Polyester thread will not take the silk dyes. For garments, you can sew with a polyester or cotton thread, although the purists will want to use silk thread to match the fabric if it is available.

Seams on most silk garments can be finished by overlocking or by stitching French seams. Some fabrics, like chiffon and georgette, fray easily so French seams make the best finish as they both give strength and enclose the edges completely. If you want a soft, draped hem on georgette or chiffon, use the narrow edge foot on the sewing machine and a close zig-zag stitch of medium length. Overlock machines can do a good rolled hem but give a closer stitch and use slightly more thread.

Machine stitch around the edge, then trim close to the edge.

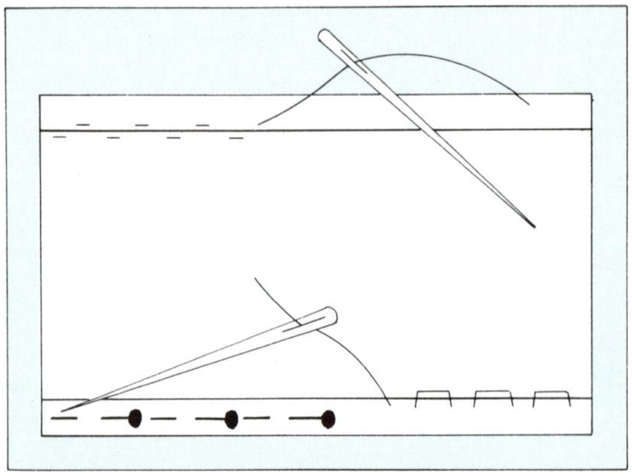

Pull stitches to create rolled hem. Finish with running stitch or blind stitch hem.

Scarf, pareo or sarong

The word 'pareo' is Tahitian in origin and means a large rectangular piece of flowered material. A 'sarong' is a similar length of fabric worn by both men and women in Malaysia and Indonesia. Pareos and sarongs are ideal for lounging around on hot summer days and nights, or worn as a beach wrap. There are many ways to wear a sarong or pareo, the style depending on the way you tie it. Therefore, they lend themselves to unusual and exotic designs that can be painted on to enhance the natural lustre of the silk. They can be elegant or fun and, because they drape without clinging to the body, you are free to use your imagination and paint a bold, colourful design that will be shown off to great effect.

A silk scarf can complement and dress up an outfit and flatter the wearer in a very special way, and a scarf is always an acceptable gift.

Silk scarves are usually made from pongee, twill or habutai, but for a very special scarf or lovely long evening shawl, try painting on crêpe de Chine or silk satin. Alternatively, soft chiffon can drape beautifully and paints up well.

The amount of fabric you require will depend on the style and use to which the scarf or sarong will be put, but a rough guide follows.

Fabrics

- Pareo or sarong: crêpe de Chine, habutai
- Scarf or shawl: pongee, twill, habutai, silk satin, crêpe de Chine, chiffon

Pareo or sarong: 112 cm × 190 cm
Long scarf: 148 cm × 27 cm
Square scarf: 70 cm × 70 cm or 90 cm × 90 cm
Shawl: 250 cm × 85 cm

Method

Finish your scarf or sarong with a hand-rolled hem if possible, it is time consuming but worth the effort for a special finish as most people treasure a hand-painted scarf. To make the sewing easier, machine stitch around the edges of the scarf first, approximately 1 cm away from the edge of the silk. Trim close to the stitching with small, sharp scissors. Go to the ironing board, attach one end firmly with pins and pull gently on the edge of the machine stitching, allowing the edge of the fabric to roll under. Press into position and pin. Hand stitch with a fine needle and silk thread using a running or blind hemming stitch. (see the diagrams on page 70.)

If you do not wish to do this, you can buy plain silk scarves already hemmed for painting, or you can finish the edges by machine. Machine hemming is quick and neat. For this use a fine ball-point needle and a stitch length of around 2.5 – 3. Roll the raw edge of the fabric under with your fingers to form a double hem and press it between your fingers as you stitch. The hem should be as fine as possible. Machine-rolled hems can be made with a special foot.

It is a good idea to machine the edges with a white silk thread before you paint the fabric, so that the thread also takes up the dyes and it blends into the whole piece.

Silk lingerie

Pure silk lingerie is very sensuous and gives a feeling of luxury. Camisoles, pyjamas and robes are frequently made from crêpe de Chine or silk satin, but habutai is also suitable.

Fabrics

- Crêpe de Chine, silk satin, habutai

A camisole or chemise cut on the straight grain of the fabric uses approximately 95 cm × 48 cm of fabric, while knickers take about 60 cm × 51 cm. If you wish to cut the camisole on the cross, which will give it a soft drape, allow at least 1 metre of the fabric.

Method

It is important to finish the lingerie well. French seams are advisable, especially on sheer fabrics. A neat way to finish around an armhole or neckline is to cut a bias binding from the same fabric. Bias binding is cut at a 45° angle to the selvedges and it should be about 2.5 cm wide. If you have to join strips of binding, do so following the line of the threads, that is, at an angle to the edge of the bias strip.

Rouleau tubes make the best shoulder straps. To make these cut a bias strip the required length and stitch into a tube with the right sides of the fabric together along the longer edge. Leave an end of the thread from the sewing and thread this onto a needle, tying it securely. Pull the needle through the tube so that the right side of the fabric shows and a rouleau is formed.

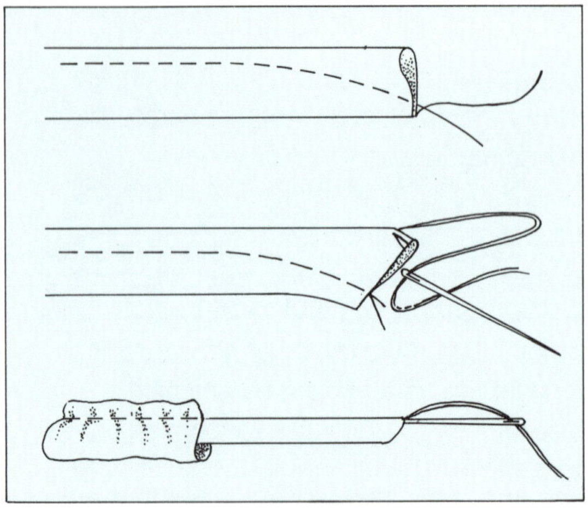

Making a rouleau tube for shoulder straps

When choosing lace for trimming lingerie, take care to select fine lace that will keep the luxurious, delicate look of the garment. Dye the lace to match with iron-on fabric paints if you cannot find the right shade.

You may wish to paint a design all over the fabric or do a single motif. If you intend to do a single motif, trace it onto the fabric with an erasable pen, having first experimented with the positioning of the design. I recommend iron-on paints rather than steam-fixed dyes for small motifs as a natural silk will go slightly cream in the steaming process.

Silk jewellery

Silk jewellery is a lovely way to use any special small pieces of hand-painted silk. Brooches, buckles and earrings can be made from experimental pieces or from offcuts of silk after you have cut out a garment – in fact, you can use any piece of silk that has interesting shapes and colours on it. You may also choose to paint a piece especially for jewellery – a delicate miniature design is ideal.

In the photograph opposite page 69, silk threads flow across a tiny painting that consists of simple shapes and soft colours.

Instructions for the brooch follow.

Fabrics

- Any fine silk such as pongee, habutai or chiffon

Method

The fragment of silk is encased between two pieces of perspex. The perspex can be held together in two ways.

1 Using some of the finely rolled copper foil that is available from specialist craft shops, carefully press the foil around the edges of the perspex, overlapping the edges by 2 mm, and gently rolling it around the corners and sides. Attach a brooch mounting with strong adhesive, such as araldite.

2 Drill four very tiny holes in the corners of the perspex and fasten the two pieces together with tiny screws. Attach a brooch mounting as described in 1 above.

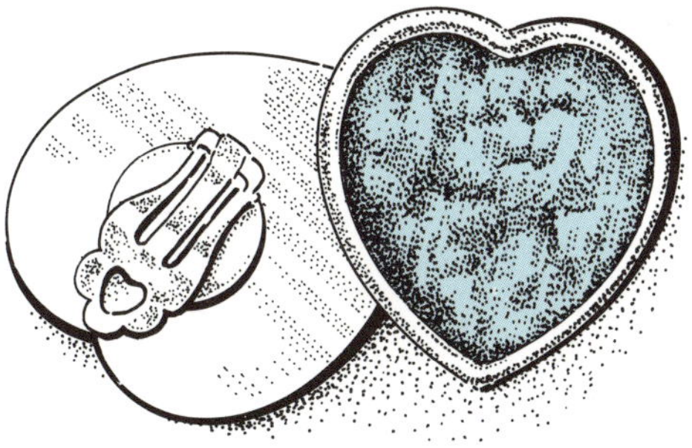

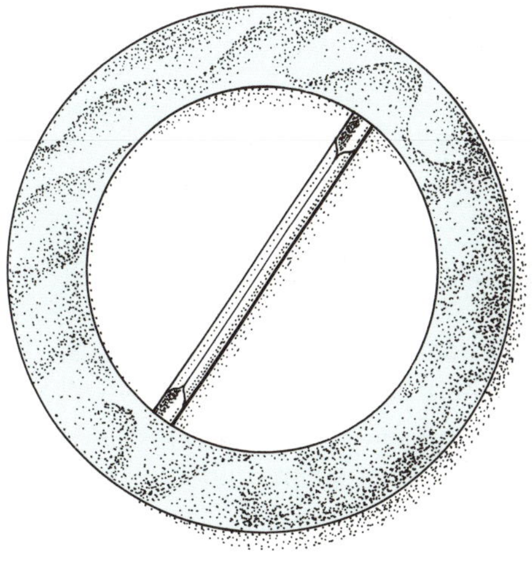

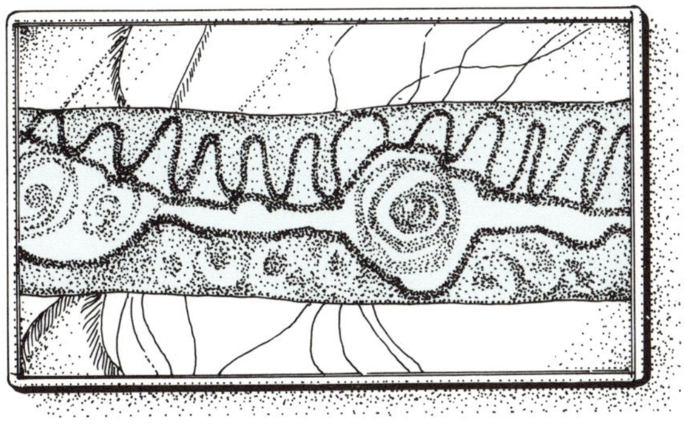

Quilted jacket

Hand-painted silk lends itself to quilting and embroidery. Quilting has been popular for centuries, and never more so than at the present time. It is an art form in itself, and one that allows for great freedom of expression.

With this jacket, illustrated in colour facing page 69, machine quilting has been chosen to give a three-dimensional quality to the design and to add warmth to the jacket.

Machine quilting is not difficult to do, but it requires patience and an eye for knowing how to get the effect that you are after – and to enhance the design by quilting the outline. When quilting a scene or gutta-edged shapes, remember not all the lines need to be stitched. Try not to over-quilt, especially if you are a beginner, as it is much easier to add to your work later than to unpick the quilting stitches. It is easiest to quilt the centre of a design first and work outwards.

Fabrics

- Habutai

The amount required will depend upon the width of the silk and the pattern you are using.

Method

1. Cut out the painted silk according to your pattern, allowing an extra 5 cm all around.
2. Place a flat layer of wadding material without any seams under the silk and cut it out as for the silk.
3. If you are using a good quality wadding you are now ready for the next step, but if the wadding is a little coarse, place a layer of pongee underneath the wadding and silk and cut it to the same size.

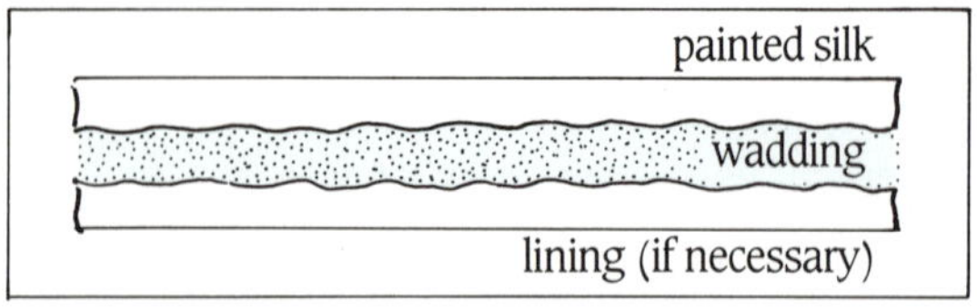

4. Tack the layers together with long tacking stitches going both horizontally and vertically across the fabric in lines about 5 cm apart.

   Alternatively, you can use a spray adhesive suitable for fabric. To do this, spray very lightly over the wadding (do *not* spray directly onto the silk). Allow it to dry. Lay the silk over the wadding, it is not necessary for the edges to adhere well, just

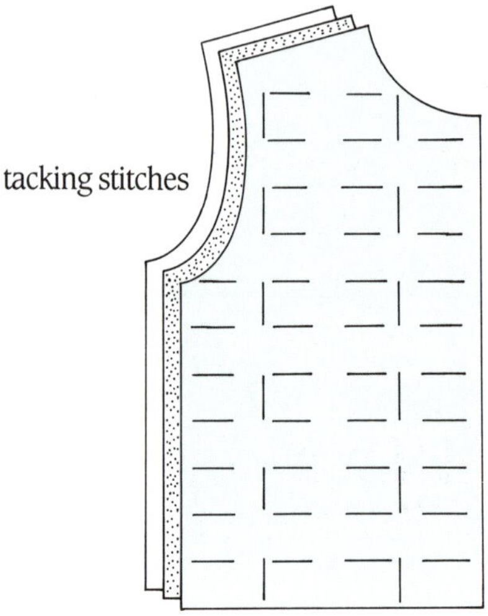

to stick so that the fabric and wadding do not move while you are stitching.

5 To quilt, machine stitch around the contours of the design. A walking foot is recommended by some machine manufacturers as it will help to prevent pulling as you stitch.

6 To make up the jacket, sew the seams together.

7 Sew the seams of the lining fabric.

8 Insert piping between the lining and the padded silk on the cuffs and outside edges of the jacket.

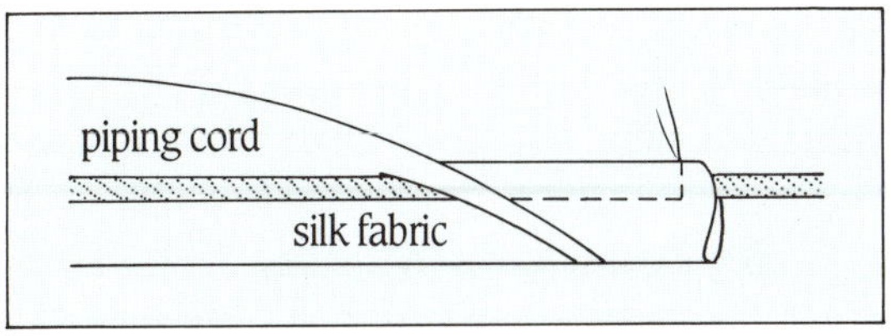

9 Stitch around the neck, front and lower edges of the jacket leaving about 20 cm open at the lower back.

10 Turn the jacket to the right side and hem the back opening closed.

The finished jacket, which is also shown in colour facing page 69.

Greeting cards

A small piece of hand-painted silk mounted as a greeting card makes an attractive and individual memento for all kinds of occasions. Mounts are available from craft shops and come in varying sizes and shapes – rectangular, oval or round – complete with a matching envelope. For a large quantity, you can order your own special design from your local printer.

Fabrics

- Any type of silk is suitable.

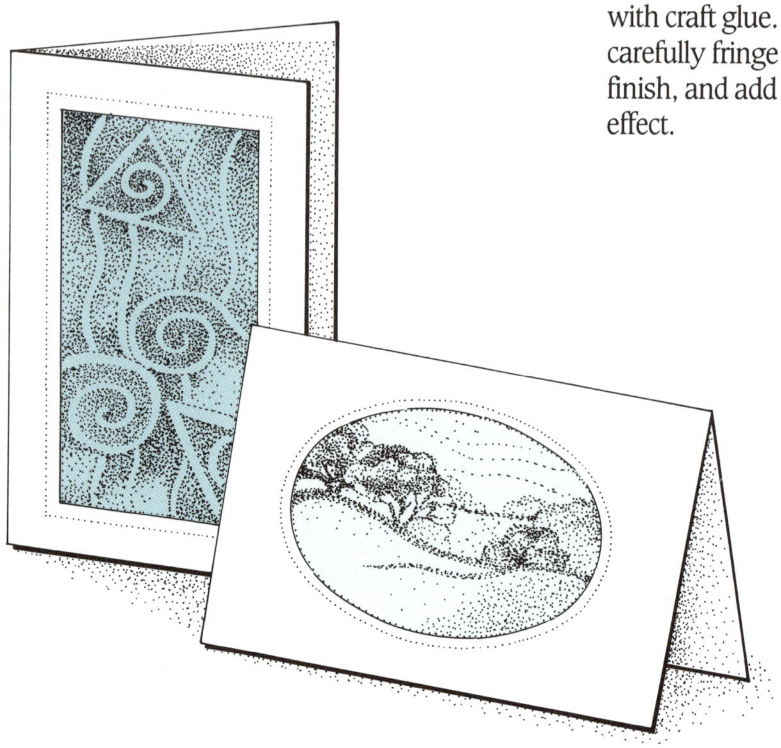

Method

1. Select the piece of painted silk that you wish to use: either an offcut with an attractive pattern or colours on it or paint your own miniature scene or design.
2. You can always decorate the silk with a few lines of metallic gutta or ink, or try stitching on a few beads.
3. If you wish to give a padded effect, cut a fine piece of wadding to exactly the shape of the hole in your card and lay it between the silk and the card.
4. The silk can be attached to the mount with double-sided tape or mounted on the front with craft glue. If attaching it to the front, carefully fringe the edges for an attractive finish, and add beads for an eye-catching effect.

SECTION 5

Appendices

FURTHER READING

Bevlin, Marjorie Elliott. *Design Through Discovery.* Holt Reinhardt Winston, USA, 1980.

Birren, Faber (ed.). *The Elements of Colour. A Treatise on the Colour System of Johannes Itten Based on his Book* The Art of Colour. Van Nostrand Reinhold Co., New York, 1970.

de Boer, Janet (ed.). *Dyeing Fibres and Fabrics.* Kangaroo Press, Kenthurst, NSW, 1987.

Franck, Frederick. *The Awakened Eye.* Vintage Books, New York, 1979.

Goldsmith, Lawrence. *Watercolour Bold and Free.* Watson-Guptill Publications, New York, 1980.

Kennedy, Jill and Varrall, Jane. *Painting on Silk.* Dryad Press, London, 1988.

Owen, Peter and Rollason, Jane. *The Complete Manual of Airbrushing Techniques.* Collins, Sydney, 1988.

Wada, Yoshiko, Rice, Mary Kellog and Barton, Jane. *Shibori: The Inventive Art of Japanese Shaped Resist Dyeing.* Kodanska International, USA, 1983.

Wilcox, Michael. *Blue and Yellow Don't Make Green.* Artways, Perth, 1987.

CONTRIBUTORS

Colleen Weste

Colleen Weste is a textile artist who has always loved colour and been fascinated with applying dyes to fibres and fabrics. Her love of colour found its 'niche' in silk painting a decade ago and she continues to create vibrant, unique fashion garments and art pieces, taking inspirations from the world of nature. Colleen has studied textiles in Australia and the United States, and she is a colour consultant and a trained teacher. Currently manager of her own retail craft business, Silk & Threads, Colleen works and lives in Melbourne. She and her husband, Ron Weste, a keen photographer, head off to the country whenever they can to photograph their environment.

Liz Darby

Liz was born in Melbourne in 1959 and has been interested in drawing and painting since childhood. She lived in a number of different places as a child, including two years in South Africa, which served to further stimulate her interest in wildlife art. Following a three year period as a zoo keeper in England (working with birds and carnivores) and three weeks touring the Kenyan game reserves, Liz spent six months travelling around the British Isles observing and sketching native wildlife in national parks and countryside areas. Since returning to Australia in 1982 and working briefly again as a zoo keeper at the Healesville Sanctuary, Liz has concentrated on developing a career as a wildlife artist. Having participated in many exhibitions, her main mediums are watercolour, oils and silk-painting.

Eleanor (Ellie) England

Ellie England was born in the United Kingdom and now lives in Victoria. She studied life drawing, painting, lithography, etching, aquatint, screen printing, fine binding, fine art printing and illustration at Plymouth College of Art and Design. She has worked in graphic design and as an art and craft teacher at secondary and tertiary levels. At present, Ellie England works in the fibre arts, silk painting, fabric design, wearable art and soft sculpture. In addition to preparing work for exhibitions and commissions, she conducts silk painting workshops. In 1990 she won an Australian Tourism Souvenir Design Award for her silk shawl *Australiana.*

Marie Ingrouille

Born in Gippsland, Marie Ingrouille gained a Diploma in Needlecraft from Emily McPherson College, Melbourne. She has tutored at the Sale Regional Continuing Education Centre Inc. in dressmaking, fashion design, embroidery and tapestry, and has conducted workshops in batik, screen printing, embroidery and silk painting. Her work has been shown in exhibitions in Victoria and examples of her work may be found at Sale Regional Arts Centre and in private collections in the United Kingdom, United States of America, Canada, Malaysia, Sweden and Australia.

Thel Merry

Thel Merry's artistic gift was recognised at a very early age, and in her early teen years she was educated in fine arts at the East Sydney Technical College. After leaving college she was chief artist for a leading Sydney company. She has taught at the Queensland College of Art, the Brisbane College of Advanced Education and the Brisbane School of Fashion for the Queensland Education Department. She also has conducted many workshops. Thel has won several awards for painting and ceramic sculpture, as well as for batik, machine embroidery and fabric art. She has exhibited her work in Brisbane, Canberra and Melbourne. At present Thel has a private studio at Montville, Queensland, and her work is represented in private collections in all states of Australia, in the United Kingdom, Hong Kong, Canada, the United States, the Bahamas, France and Italy.

Robin Rogerson

Robin Rogerson was born in New Zealand. She has studied Chinese painting in Hong Kong and European techniques in Wellington and Melbourne. Her work has been exhibited both overseas and in Australia, including several solo exhibitions. In addition, Robin's work is represented in private and corporate collections around the world.

SUPPLIERS

New South Wales

Batik Oetoro (wholesale and retail)
203 Avoca Street
Randwick 2034
02 398 6201

Silk Express and full range of textile dyes.

South Australia

Commission Dyers Pty Ltd
7 Pinn Street
St Marys 5042
08 276 2844

Dyes for silk, cotton and wool.

Marie-France
92 Currie Street
Adelaide 5000
08 231 4138

Leprince (French) and Deka (German) dyes.

Victoria

Francheville (wholesale)
1 Perry Street
Collingwood 3630
03 416 0611

Pebeo Orient Express and Setacolour.

Kraftkolour (wholesale and retail)
Factory 11/72 Chifley Drive
Preston 3072
03 484 4303

Procion, Drimalan, Drimarene dyes.

Marie-France
223 High Street
Kew 3101
03 862 2668

Leprince (French) and Deka (German) dyes.

Silk & Threads (wholesale and retail)
132 Martin Street
Gardenvale 3185
03 596 1783

Dupont, Drimalan and Dekasilk dyes.

Zart Art (wholesale to schools and retail)
Factory 4/41 Lexton Road
Box Hill North 3129
03 890 1869

Dupont, Pebeo dyes and textile paints.

INDEX

References in **bold** type relate to colour plates.